ADVANCE PRAISE FOR *AM I CRAZY?*

"Chad is a verbal cannon with common sense. He calls things as they are and sees the serious issues with a humorous slant. Regardless of what side you stand on, he shines a spotlight on the cultural condition and helps us remember that we are all just humble human beings navigating the journey called life."

GLENN BECK, *New York Times* Bestselling Author
and Host, *The Glenn Beck Program*

"This book is classic Chad Prather, which is to say insightful, manly, funny—absolute must read!"

DINESH D'SOUZA, *New York Times* Bestselling Author
of *United States of Socialism*

"In a time when we are constantly lectured by powerful elites, Chad Prather brings a much-needed commonsense sanity to the political landscape. I unapologetically endorse this patriot."

DAVE RUBIN, *New York Times* Bestselling Author
of *Don't Burn This Book*

"It's been said that common sense isn't so common anymore, and that's exactly why the world needs Chad Prather more than ever. He's a throwback to a saner and more fun-loving America. His rants are OUR rants. So if you're not sure whether to laugh or cry when you turn on the news, read this book and be consoled in knowing these woke radicals have provided Chad with a ton of fodder for some amazing jokes."

CHARLIE KIRK, National Radio Host and Founder
of Turning Point USA

"Chad's wisdom has an easy place between a fine bourbon and a laugh in the kind of way that makes you think 'Am I getting old, because this used to make sense.' You're not getting old. You're just enjoying the personality of someone who makes the crazy talk around you feel less crazy."

ANDREW WILKOW, Host, *The Wilkow Majority*

"Chad Prather is the Will Rogers of our time: funny, thoughtful, and quintessentially American. If that appeals to you, so will this book. Buy it, laugh, and enjoy his unique perspective on America."

LARRY ALEX TAUNTON, Author of
Around the World in (More Than) 80 Days

"Chad has perfected his storytelling ability using both historical references and humor to drive a point home. Societal issues may seem complicated, but Chad is masterful at quickly simplifying even the most complex of issues. *Am I Crazy?* is a breath of fresh air in a time where everyone else is too afraid to speak the truth. Who knew a redneck could be so insightful?!"

SARA GONZALES, Host, Blaze TV's *The News and Why It Matters*

"Chad uses his humor and amazing way to connect with Americans to make sense of the crazy times we are in. Whether you love him or hate him, we need more people just like him. We are in a fight for America, and I'm glad we have Chad Prather's *Am I Crazy?!*"

GRAHAM ALLEN, Founder of Nine Twelve United
and Author of *America 3:16*

AM I CRAZY?

AM I CRAZY?

An *Unapologetic* Patriot
Takes on the Insanity
of Today's Woke World

★ CHAD PRATHER ★

Humanix Books
www.humanixbooks.com

Humanix Books

AM I CRAZY?
Copyright © 2021 by Chad Prather
All rights reserved

Humanix Books, P.O. Box 20989, West Palm Beach, FL 33416, USA
www.humanixbooks.com | info@humanixbooks.com

Humanix Books is a division of Humanix Publishing, LLC. Its
trademark, consisting of the words "Humanix Books," is registered in
the Patent and Trademark Office and in other countries.

ISBN: 9-781-63006-205-7 (Hardcover)
ISBN: 9-781-63006-206-4 (E-book)

Printed in the United States of America
10 9 8 7 6 5 4 3 2 1

This book is dedicated to my parents,
Pete and Gloria Prather.
They say that a person is formed by
both genetics and environment.
Thanks Mom and Dad for
making me wonderfully crazy.

Contents

PART II: RANTS ON CULTURE
Our Demented Drama   89

PART III: RANTS ON MARRIAGE, RELATIONSHIPS, AND FAMILY
A Crazy Mystery   155

Foreword

Of course Chad is crazy. He's gone and put all his non-sense in a book. He never listens. I used to tell him during his rebellious teenage years that while I loved him, I didn't have to *like* him. A little bit of tough love (his father and I beat his butt), and he turned out reasonably okay. He's still crazy, though. Why anyone would post their entire life and personal business online for the world to see like he does is beyond my imagination. When I first heard that he'd gone "viral," I just assumed he'd gotten sick. Now I know he's just sick in the head—and sharing it with the general public. Maybe that's why he's one of the better voices to deal with the insanity of today's crazy world. I mean, have you ever seen such nonsense? I guess the world needs more of Chad's type of craziness to bring us back into balance. Don't tell him I said that. He will only remind me I said it whenever I tell him to hush. Enjoy the book. Don't blame me. I can still beat his butt!

—Gloria, Chad's Mom

World Gone Crazy

Is it just me, or has the whole world gone crazy? I'm no Luddite, and I'm not necessarily adversarial to the modern age, but I find myself pining for the world of yesteryear. And I don't mean some idealized, romanticized, sugar-coated version of the 1940s and 1950s, where you could get your best girl a malt from the local soda jerk for a nickel or the kids couldn't wait till next week to hear if Little Orphan Annie was going to survive the cliffhanger. I'm talking about the real world of only a couple decades ago. Sometime in the 1990s maybe. Perhaps one week in June of '91. A small window but nonetheless. Back when people weren't offended every time the winds of culture blew in a perceived disagreeable direction. Before victimhood was considered a virtue and hard work actually resulted in success and not shelves filled with participation trophies. You know, back when the Karate Kid stood up and kicked and kicked that asshole Johnny in the face and we all cheered.

Yes! America!!!

Back when you could laugh at an Eddie Murphy stand-up routine without feeling the need to retreat to your safe space, suck your thumb, while rocking back and forth in the corner humming "Jesus Loves Me." Back before words like "woke" appeared, and we didn't really care what a "beta male" was. Back before masculinity got labeled toxic and you could flirt with a girl in public. Oh hell no! Those days are long gone.

The way it appears to me, the world has closed its eyes, taken a flying leap, and plunged headfirst down the weirdest Slip 'N Slide imaginable, to the point that up and down, right and wrong, in and out no longer mean anything in the new paradigm from which we view our existence as a species. The idea of "my truth" has replaced actual truth. Your character is now judged by how you use certain words in your vocabulary. You can find yourself immediately labeled and "canceled" in one amazingly mistaken grammatical error. In short, people have lost their damn minds.

We used to celebrate the accomplishments and growth of mankind. Remember us? Mankind? The sole owner and proprietor of advanced abstract reasoning on this old blue and green marble called Earth. We have traded in our intellectual birthright and ability to think critically for a bowl of pureed, platitudinal meme-think and social media mental mush. We don't think for ourselves anymore because—let's face it—thinking is hard. We've been so busy keeping up with the Kardashians, rewriting history, and banning certain words from our language that we have no identity beyond our own self-perceived sense of suffering and persecution. Social media has canned our collective consciousness and stored it in the proverbial cellar for use at some uncertain future date, and we stare on haplessly with drool slowly pooling beneath the grins on our skulls that contain a seemingly lobotomized frontal lobe.

I guess we now take pride in being dumbasses.

Which brings me back to my original point: We are crazy. Who the hell is content to consistently bathe in the ignorance of today's crazy thinking? Social media just serves to give you a bigger daily heaping spoonful of stupid. We gobble up dumb opinions, fake news, clickbait, and online pablum like a fat kid who just got permission to come off Michelle Obama's school lunch diet.

Don't get me wrong. I'm crazier than you because I've chosen to use the internet—specifically social media—to build a career in entertainment. I was able to figure out a way to take the sociological experiment they call Facebook and YouTube and actually use them to make a profit. I may have shaved years off my life in so doing, but kudos to my crazy ass for hanging in there tighter than a hair in a biscuit.

For years people have introduced me as an "internet sensation," which is just a twenty-first-century way of describing someone who is actually unemployed but really popular. Who knows? My very concerned mother called me a few years ago wanting to know if I was sick because she'd heard from someone that I "went viral." I informed her that they were only talking about my Facebook and my Twitter feeds, to which she clutched her pearls and replied, "Chad! You're 43! You shouldn't be touching your Twitter!" Of course, at that point I didn't have the nerve to tell her about my Snapchat. Nevertheless, here I am, swimming in the deep end of the cultural cesspool that is social media.

Why Does Recognizing Our Crazy Matter?

Throughout history, people have recorded their lives on walls. From Egyptian hieroglyphics to native cave drawings, thousand-year-old stories of humanity have been kept for posterity. Today we record our stories on a digital wall. And trust me, our craziness is not only recorded, it's there forever! Historically, we only held onto the words of the smart people—you know, the priests, poets, prophets, philosophers, kings, and so forth.

Well . . . those days are long gone.

Any moron with a keyboard is given a platform to place his or her words and musings on the digital wall for everyone to see. Yep. We have gone crazy, and we have it on full display. Every day. Little attention addicts with crazy thoughts rattling around in our skulls like bowling pins.

In the following pages I can't wait to prove this to you. We are going to walk through the crazy patterns of life in America: love and marriage, parenting, the personalities that steal our attention, and the random hodgepodge of demented drama that's being paraded as normal behavior. It's not. It's crazy.

Padded cells be dammed; the asylums are empty, and the insanity is on full display. We aren't flying over the cuckoo's nest. We sitting right in the middle of it with all the other crazy eggs. It's going to be like taking Viagra . . . but for your brain. 'Cause everyone needs a hard brain. Or something like that. Either way, right now it's flaccid and mushy. I'm here to change that—or maybe I'm just crazy.

Join me on a journey. These last few years have been one big roller coaster of emotions. I've done my best to collect my random musings on topical issues when they happened and even as they happened. Try as we may, things are changing so fast it's hard to keep up. Here's my attempt to make sense of all the insanity of the last few years.

A Note to Liberals

Hi, liberals. My name is Chad Prather, and you may have heard of me. I'm that guy you've seen—despite your best efforts—on Facebook and YouTube, sitting in his truck and talking in a thick (and may I say lovely) southern drawl about everything that triggers you: from the breakdown of traditional American Judeo-Christian values to the MAGA hat–wearing awesomeness of Donald Trump; from the reality of beautiful and important differences between the genders to the fact that for the life of me, I don't know if I hate anything as much as I hate skinny jeans. There, I said it.

In other words, I'm just your friendly neighborhood cowboy hat–wearing, politically and culturally conservative, fast-talking cowboy from Texas. Undoubtedly, I am known among your circles as a fascist, Nazi, homophobic, misogynistic bigot with racist overtones and xenophobic undertones. No doubt you are of the opinion that I spend every day beating my wife, dumping burning coals on homeless people, and launching illegal immigrants back across the Rio Grande with a catapult (in truth, I only do one of those things per day). And if the only reason you're reading this is that it's among the stack of books you're about to throw on the bonfire, let me quickly tell you three things:

1. Burning books emits carbon, and you're going to liberal hell for that (of course, not burning my book probably sends you to the same place, so you're damned if you do and damned if you don't).
2. If you do burn this book, please continue buying more copies and burning them as well. I wouldn't want my message to get out—so do your duty! Granted, this could create more catharsis in your progressive mind because you would be utilizing capitalism, but I'm personally okay with the "buy and burn" censorship method.
3. I like you.

Yeah, that last one's a little tricky, isn't it? If you're a dyed-in-the-wool liberal, the concept of liking someone you disagree with is hard to wrap your noodle around. But it's true. You're a human being, and God made you in His image every bit as much as He made me. I make it a policy in my life not to hate anyone, even liberals. Besides, if you don't agree with the things I say, that's fine: this is America, and you're allowed to be wrong as much and as often as you want.

Here's the bottom line: Take a quick peek to your right. Now to your left. See any other liberals watching you? No? Then why don't you just give this book a chance and read a little bit. You might find yourself laughing here and there. Hell, you might find yourself agreeing with a thing or two that I have to say.

Stranger things have happened.

A Note to Conservatives

You know the drill. Read and enjoy! ★

AM I CRAZY?

PART I

RANTS
ON POLITICS

We Are All
Batshit Crazy

What Crawled Up Your Butt and Died?

You mad, bro? If ever a loaded question rolled off the tongue of one human being in the general direction of another, that's it. It's only three syllables, but in response to it you're apt to get anything from a tongue lashing all the way to shot for your trouble. And, as we all know, this is especially true of people who interact on social media. No question about it: People are pissed off these days. Their angst is palpable. And why? The answer is not simple. Let me give you an example to break it down. You know that feeling you get when you're barreling down the road—just listening to a little John Denver tune about the peace and harmony of nature or smoking weed or whatever the hell he was singing about—and suddenly some bat-out-of-hell ass-hat cuts out in front of you at an equally illegal pace? You know the erudite language that involuntarily ejaculates forth out of your mouth like a wad of hot greased lightning? You know how you would never in a million years talk that way to the person's face. At least most of you, anyway? Well . . . It's something like that. Instead of road rage, we have cyber rage. We've lost our cognitive ability to communicate beyond the level of a 13-year-old schoolboy teaching other kids on the playground how to cuss.

So here we are. We have all heard the road rage analogy applied to social media, and I think we can wrap our heads collectively around the notion that when you don't stand much of a chance being caught, you feel a lot freer to express emotions you wouldn't otherwise express. But why is that rage there? It just bubbles under the surface like the puke you had to take that time you accidentally swallowed a plug of Copenhagen snuff. And by the way, why is it so much worse when we're pirouetting through that placid poppy-populated paradise that is social media? If road rage is the occasional bump of cocaine for the demonic soul that lingers within us all to one degree or another, social media is a full-on rehab-worthy addiction!

For starters, I think that social media confers a couple of things on us that we didn't used to have—a version of fame and a version of authority . . . both largely unearned. It gives us a platform from which to preach our dictums to the world, shouting them at the top of our keyboards like the cyberpunk sages we've all become—monastics in the ether of the ethernet, chanting our litany to a god that never coalesced properly in the first place.

When people go to post things on social media outlets—or, God help us, when they comment on something someone else has posted—they're wading in, by and large, with an air of artificial profundity and authority. How do I know this? Because I've seen it . . . and because I've done it. We all have. If you're on Facebook or Twitter and you've never once posted or commented on something you were not an expert on, I don't believe in you.

In the last few years, every person online has fancied themselves everything from a political science expert to an acclaimed virologist. Be more like me. I readily admit that I don't know squat.

What happens when millions of people all hop on a platform where they are expected (or at least where they expect themselves) to be an expert in something they're not? Well, did you ever have that friend who told stories that just couldn't be true? And no matter what you'd say to him, he'd just keep dying on that hill and insisting that he really did the thing you know he didn't do? It's kind of like that. Most people would cut their own arms off before admitting to anything that's going to make them sound stupid. It really is okay to realize that you don't know something. To continue to build on the fallacy that you do just further solidifies your standing in the nuthouse.

These things start to build on each other. We "troll," we "own," we "destroy," we "ratio" one another with memes and poorly spelled screeds written in the dim emojic hieroglyphs of our dying language because it is the way that we maintain that measure of fame and authority. And then we begin to feed off the anger itself—it becomes a kind of intellectual comfort food. You're going to feel good when you eat it, but it'll give you a fat and bloated head.

Soon you will trade all critical and complex thinking skills for really fabulous thumb muscles from pooling all your ignorance online. Hey! I know. I'm guilty.

Now, to be fair, there are plenty of things and opinions in the world that should make you mad. I don't want to chalk everything up to us being silly people who do silly things. Sometimes someone posts something morally execrable or otherwise odious, and it isn't just okay to be pissed off at it—you pretty much have to be. And sometimes—not often, but sometimes—whatever it is even warrants you wading in shit deep into the crazy pool to make your objection known. (But really, how often are you going to change a person's mind on social media? Has it ever happened to you?)

I think the question we've got to ask ourselves is simple: When we see something and feel the old blood beginning to boil, can we ask ourselves, "Am I mad for the right reason? Am I justified in feeling this way? And if I am, what's the most appropriate way for me to respond to it?" This seems sane enough. Unfortunately, we have already fired off our salvo before we even begin to question our motives and purpose. We just need to be heard and justified, dammit. We are so crazy.

Here's an interesting little concept for you to think about: In the world of psychotherapy, it's said that there is no such thing as the emotion called "anger." There is only some combination of the emotions "sad" and "scared." So every situation in which you find yourself pissed off about something, what's really going on is that you're part sad about something, part scared about it, or both. I waver on whether or not to think that this is completely true, but it's a good platform on which to dissect this little outrage problem we seem to have in this country.

And listen, even if you ask yourself those questions and manage to get your own backyard cleaned up, you're never going to pull every mouth off the gigantic social media teat all at once—there's just too many people out there lapping up that delicious, delicious rage!

Are You Woke Enough?

Welcome to the wondrous wide world of "wokeism," fellow enemies of privilege living in a world where Donald Trump became president of the United States and drove the world batshit crazy over it! I am your chief interlocutor, your elocutionist extraordinaire, and I will sign legal documents to the effect that I will nonthreateningly hold your hand as we skip through the field of daisies and unicorns that we all know will be possible when we finally remove all white cisgender male privilege from the face of the Earth. My sweet allies against white colonialism, I have summarily removed my testicles and deposited them at the feet of a half-black, half-Asian transgender female Ivy League professor of gender studies so that she may step on them and gain further empowerment in a world that has held her down for so long!

I am *woke*! Mine eyes have seen the glory of the coming of social justice in all things. And if you haven't gained such a spectacular vision of the way the world should be, then there's something wrong with you. You should be triggered, but wait . . .

My question to you today is not, *Are you triggered?*, but *Are you triggered enough?*! Fellow soldiers in the Social Justice War, it is time not to "man" our battle stations but to "person" them. My antifascist friends out there, for too long you have fought alone against racist, sexist, bigoted, ableist, misogynist, homophobic, and transphobic Nazis who occupy both this country and, formerly, its White House. (Shudder) Even the term *White House* is a microaggression to me! We have to join together to make the world a better place.

Are you triggered enough? We live in a world where devastating gender inequality exists right alongside the stone-cold fact that gender is a social construct and isn't real! How is it that white cisgender males can even take something that isn't real and appropriate it for themselves?!

Listen up all you hashtag-o-sexual, spotted owl–defending sign bearers of doom. While you're marching around wearing your thick-rimmed glasses, your uggo camouflage, and your pink hats displaying that the only thing you got rollin' around your noggin is prefrontal labia, the rest of us are out here in the real world, trying our best to objectively describe what we see around us so as to be able to construct better dialogue with our fellow man. And yes, I said *man*. Go ahead. I'll give you a couple seconds to scream at the sky.

Listen, I'm as big a fan of slingin' around Sunday words as anyone else, but this language of *woke* that you speak with such fervor is a giant running-sore-like symptom of the intellectual disease known as "false acumen." The natural dissemination of concepts like "the patriarchy" is the worst kind of game to have to watch from the sidelines because it creates an inaccurate sense of thoughtful profundity. What it's really doing under the surface, though, is constructing a Rube Goldberg–like labyrinthine machine of coat-hanger phrases upon which to rest your emotions. But it seems that to you—the *woke* left—this is a feature and not a bug. Gone are the days of rational discourse, because in this new world of false acumen, the goal is never to be the most logical voice in the room but instead to be the most passionate. In short, to use one of your own terms against you, the ideological construct that is woke leftism is logic-adjacent.

George Orwell is the over-referenced and under-studied hero of everyone who only dips an occasional toe into the waters of political rhetoric, but he did envision a world in which the expressed goal of the vocal majority was to excise all thought from language while retaining its passion in a guttural form. I hate to be the doomsday cowboy, but you could do worse than to brush up on your *1984* reading—we ain't that far out from what he was predicting.

Folks, don't be fooled by the synthetic wisdom displayed in our current catchphrase culture. Remember that behind every well-crafted parcel of human speech, there should be something of substance. And if there isn't . . . well, you may just be talking to a liberal.

And to my liberal friends out there—if you take nothing else away from what I'm sayin', take this: start thinking through some of this stuff you're saying. Don't just repeat what's been passed down to you from the collegiate minds on high—they don't always know what they're talking about. Of course, neither do I . . . but I can admit it. ★

Which Idiot Is the Victor, and Why Is He Writing History?

Somewhere near the Mediterranean Sea, circa the fifth century BC, the Greeks and the Persians were about to go to war. Now if you've ever seen a schoolyard fight, you know how most of these things begin: with the trash-talking, right? And I sometimes like to think about how that might have gone down. Could've been a little like this . . .

PERSIAN: I'm about to whip your butt.

GREEK: I'm sorry, I couldn't hear you through these awesome locks of beautiful hair. What did you say?

PERSIAN: I said, I'm about to whip your butt.

GREEK: Oh, that's cute, but I don't really have time for that today—I've got an appointment at Hair-Cropolus. How's Tuesday for you?

PERSIAN: Stupid Greek! I'm going to raze your cities to the ground! I'm going to have my way with all your women— except the uggos—and sell all your children into slavery! I will wipe your civilization from the face of the Earth!

GREEK: Yeah, yeah, tons of arrows and us fighting in the shade and all that jazz. Look, you lost half your ships just getting here. And you think you're just gonna march your janky butt over hundreds of miles of rocky terrain and beat us at the home stadium? You're wearing sandals, mother-effer! You're gonna stub all ten toes the first day!

PERSIAN: Listen here, you skirt-wearing sissy—when we win, I'm gonna tell everyone how light in the sandals you are. The whole world's going to know about the Greeks!

GREEK: Those are fighting words!

Okay, so maybe that's how it went down, and maybe it isn't. The point is, something we don't stop to think about often enough is who writes history. Who wrote what we learned when we were growing up, who's writing it now, and—maybe scariest of all—who's going to write about our present day when that becomes history?

I've been more than a little dismayed to see the systematic dismantling of the American story as it existed when I was growing up. I mean, it's one thing to update details as we go along— sometimes you really do find out that something you thought happened didn't. George Washington, for instance, actually did not chop down a cherry tree. But it's something else entirely when you have people whose goal it is to completely uproot and destroy the American mythos. It has become fashionable in our society to hate ourselves and to hate our history, and that's a direct result of the cancer of being *woke* spreading throughout the American body politic and metastasizing in our collective consciousness.

We valiantly embrace being woke with open arms and a mind so open that our brains are falling out—but it's the kiss of death for our society. Get woke and be weak because being woke never works. It crucifies the individual, his or her thinking and speech, in the name of redeeming our supposedly narrow-minded culture. But beware! In October 2019, even former U.S. President Barack Obama made comments that critiqued woke culture, stating, "This idea of purity and you're never compromised and you're politically woke, and all that stuff—you should get over that quickly. The world is messy. There are ambiguities. People who do really good stuff have flaws."

People are at a point where they actually want America to fail because of some self-imposed sense of sadomasochistic guilt. We are now taught that the very foundation of this country rests upon racism, bigotry, and the selfish evil scourge of capitalism (you know, that economic system that lifted half the world's population out of desperate poverty over the past few decades and literally created a thing called the *American dream*?). We're coming to learn that America didn't start in 1776 with the Declaration of Independence but rather that it started in 1619 with the founding of Jamestown and the apparent advent of abhorrent slavery upon our shores. We're told that this country was built entirely on the backs of slaves. The contributions of hardworking Americans other than slaves, the bravery and devotion to ideals higher than themselves held by the nation's Founders, the adventurous nature of the pioneers who struck off into a dangerous country overwhelmingly sparsely populated—all these things are not only being backed into the corner of history, but in fact, they're being eradicated piecemeal by the new historical understanding that's emerging from the woke subculture.

Now here's my thing: I love everybody, and I'm perfectly willing for some jackass to think whatever he, she, or zir wants to think about how this country came to be. Part of living in a free society is accepting that there are going to be ignoramuses out there, and they can think what they want. But I draw a line when it gets to the point that they want to fill my kids' heads with this nonsense. And folks, we're already there. We were there decades ago—it just wasn't as bad yet. But as the great preacher and orator John Wesley once said, "What one generation tolerates, the next will embrace." History is always, always, always under attack—make no mistake. But it gets worse over time before it eventually gets better, and we're in the part of the cycle where it's still getting worse. Look, you don't have to worship at the feet of the American Founders to realize that what they set in motion was an experiment in freedom that—while imperfect and quite fragile—nevertheless sought and still seeks to always be more perfect. And you don't have to believe that America has always gotten things right—or even always gets them right now—to understand that it is a fundamentally good place, the best place in fact.

So the real question here is, what are we gonna do about all this? If the Wokie McWokersons of the country have their way, we won't have an America pretty soon. The whole Orwellian notion that the person who controls the past controls the present is all too true, and it seems like in some dim, instinctual way, the woke crowd gets that. So it's incumbent upon us to take a page from their book—or maybe to take a page from the book they stole from us. Here's the deal: what do you think Joe and Jane WokeFace are telling their children (you know, the ones they didn't abort) about American history? More important, do you think that they're just assuming that those kids will pick up all the historical education they need from school? I guarantee you the answer is no—AND THEY HAVE THE ADVANTAGE BECAUSE THE SCHOOL'S

ON THEIR SIDE! Those parents are making sure every day to coach their kids in the ways of woke, and that includes making sure that their version of history lines up with woke orthodoxy.

It's time that we started doing the same with our own children, and really with ourselves. I hate to give you all homework, but we can't avoid it: we're going to have to read, and we're going to have to make sure that our kids read. The real history of America is still out there—they haven't managed to burn it all yet. And while it's still there, we have to instill it and install it in our heads and in the heads of our kids. Because one day, those little mouth breathers of ours are going to inherit this country, and I don't know about you, but I want them to know where it came from and what to do with it when they do.

So even if you are a fan of history, you can always learn more. Get to reading, and get those kids to reading as well. ★

Independently Insane

L et's talk about the Fourth of July for a few minutes. For anyone out there who doesn't know—and there can't be many of you, because we're pretty loud and proud about it—if the United States of America was a religion, the Fourth of July would be our Easter. It's a day when we celebrate several things at once, and we honor those who sacrificed sometimes literally everything to bring us to where we are today. Number one, we celebrate the day that we Americans declared our independence from Britain and subsequently kicked their butt in a war. Hashtag sorry-not-sorry, Britain. We also celebrate the formation of the greatest country with the greatest form of government—of the people, by the people, for the people—in the history of the entire world. A country which, by the way, has fought for the freedom of millions of other people around the world and lifted millions more out of desperate poverty. Finally, and most important, we celebrate when Will Smith and Jeff Goldblum planted a nuclear bomb aboard the space alien mothership using a computer virus to hack into the ship's security. On that day, just like President Bill Pullman said, we stood up as a united human race and told the aliens that we will not go quietly into the night. We will not go down without a fight! We're going to live on! This is our Independence Day!

Okay, so maybe that last part was a movie. But the rest of it's true, and it really is the heart of what unites us as a country. In the steamy doldrums of the summer of 1776, the fathers and mothers of our country stood up and announced to the world that in this new nation, man as an individual would be sovereign—that self-determination was to be the order of the new world. Two hundred and forty-four years later, we Americans inhabit the world that that philosophy built. It's a damn fine place to live, folks. And even though we're also experiencing the most divisive time politically since the days leading up to the Civil War, the truth of the matter is that we are still a united people. Sure, you've got some idiots on the fringes, and sure they've got a helluva bullhorn in the form of the mainstream media and social media, but the truth of the matter is that they are the vocal minority. They are loud, and they can be powerful, but only if we continue to let them be.

Folks, the things that bind us as Americans vastly outweigh the things that divide us—always have. Why the hell do you think so many people are trying to get in? Why can't we get any celebrities to leave?

You want to know what the fastest way to get folks at the southern border to turn around probably is? Go down there and convince them that our country is the same as their country. The last thing you'll see is their shoulders sagging as they turn tail and head back.

We are united by our freedom. Even if it's a freedom to be jerks. Our extreme liberty exists on a world stage where such a thing has rarely existed at all and has never existed with such totality. Most of us recognize the gravity of that freedom, and nearly all of us honor the men and women who face down tyranny up to and including the expense of their own lives so that we can all continue to live in the manner to which we've become accustomed. The Fourth of July exists as a holiday, not so we can blow our fingers off after screaming, "Hey y'all, watch this," but because it's a chance for us to revel in the life that was built for us on the backs of heroes. At least once a year, we can pause to reflect on the primary thing that brings us all together as a people—liberty!

So reach out and give your Democrat friends a hug today, folks. They might not like it, and they might start to sizzle if you're wearing a cross necklace—so take that off first—but in the end, it'll be good for both of you. Because we really *are* one nation, under God, indivisible, with liberty and justice for all. God bless America and be careful blowin' stuff up out there. Just remember when you put your head down at the end of the night to sleep that you live in the greatest place on Earth at the greatest time in history and that you should desire that blessing of freedom for everyone else.

Except for space aliens. Screw those guys. ★

What If God Is Woke

And lo, it came to pass that the kingdom of man did enter into the time of the Great Judgment, and darkness fell upon the land. And from above there came the sound of a trumpet calling, and the heavens parted—the seas dried up and the mountains were torn asunder, and there was much fear and trembling. And from the heavens there descended a golden staircase—and lo, upon its sides were flags of many colors. And it came to pass that God (pronouns Am/Are) came down the staircase, returning unto Am's people at last. And behold, the Lord God, as it turned out, was a gender fluid demipansexual upon Mondays, Wednesdays, and Fridays and a panromantic gray-sexual the other days of the week (except for the week immediately following Labor Day and all of Black History Month, during which Am would become a metronome of cis and trans demiboy throughout the whole day).

And behold, there stood upon the face of the Earth a lone cowboy—a student of philosophy and comedy—and he did look upon the face of God and the figure of Am, and his knees did weaken, for he realized too late that God was *woke*. And in an instant, the Earth did open up, and the cowboy did fall down the chasm toward Hades and did scream "Ain't that a biiiiiitch?!" on his way down. And then did he rest in the halls of his fathers.

And then God did turn Am's face upon the rest of the whole world and did smile. And Am waved Am's hand, and behold—the number of Starbucks coffee shops did immediately double on the face of the Earth. And crappy, whiny European music did resonate upon the very air. And verily, every E, Ey, Tho, Hir, Hu, Per, Thon, Jee, Ve, Xe, Ze, Zhe, and Zir with blue hair upon one side of the head and a shaven surface upon the other did fall to their knees in supplication and repentance—for God was also black.

"Rise, my children," God said, "look upon my face, and see me to be the very embodiment of everything you hold dear in this world and the world beyond! Behold, send to me your wisest, darkest minorities, and I shall have palaver with them—for lo, I bring you new language and a never-ending series of new commandments . . . which thou shall call the Woke Commandments. And thou shalt use them to root out the racism inherent in your fellow people, and thou shalt destroy them—by fire, by torture, by rending them asunder in the town square. And in doing so, thou shalt make of them an example of what happens to those who are intolerant in this, my blessed Kingdom."

And behold, God did cease speaking for a moment. And heads were bowed, and Hacky Sacks were stilled for a moment, and a great swelling of self-righteousness could be smelt upon the very air.

"To begin," God did continue, "thou shalt all put on the pink pussyhats, which show thy devotion unto me."

"But Lord God!" cried a voice from the wilderness, and all turned to look. It was neither man nor woman, but some creature from the gulf between the two lands. "Dost thou not care that in putting upon ourselves the pussyhat, we are marginalizing the plight of the transgendered among us?! Woe is me! Better that I live the rest of mine days besotted with sackcloth and ashes! Hearest thou me not, O Lord?!"

And God did smile upon the weird little creature and did hold forth one of the knit pussyhats.

"Behold," said Am, "wist thou not that upon this *pussy hat* there is sewn a long pink penis as well? Yea, verily, he/she/zhir who putteth this hat upon the head will not only be a wearer of the pussyhat, but will indeed be a dickhead as well."

The wanderer from the desert looked through tears upon the pussyhat, and indeed saw that a cloth penis did protrude and did burst gratefully into tears.

"Awww, *hell* no!" came the voice of the cowboy, from deep inside the pit. ★

The Second Amendment

Brothers and sisters, I come to you today with an opening by one of the greater sages of our day. The fallen hero Uncle Ben, from the Spider-Man series, once said, "With great power comes great responsibility."

Now it's come to my attention that this past Saturday, a Texas man—who was angry about the haircut his son had received—proceeded to shoot the barber who had done the deed. Let me repeat that for those of you who either just dropped this book or took an involuntary hiccup: a man shot a barber who had given his son a bad haircut. Say what you want about the great state of Texas—we don't fool around.

I'll tell you, I've had my fair share of bad haircuts over the course of my life, and never once have I thought to feed the barber a lead sandwich when the doing was done. I've always found it better to bust out a cap to cover the barber's mistake than to bust one in the barber himself, if you catch my drift. I mean, I suppose it'd be one thing if you asked for a high-and-tight and walked out of the store with a mullet. But even that business-in-the-front, party-in-the-back doesn't give you the right to try to smoke a guy who happened to bring a shaving razor to a gunfight. Hell, all you've got to do to get rid of what I like to call the "Missouri compromise" is a little snip-snip to the back of the dome.

Thankfully, our illustrious barber managed to make it to the hospital and is expected to pull through. There isn't anything sadder I can think of than a barbershop sextet singing "Swing Low, Sweet Chariot" while hauling a pine box down to the hearse.

So why am I telling you about this? I'll tell you why. Because if you hear anything *at all* about this shooting in the major news—and you probably won't because the shooter was a Black man—the first and only conclusion of the mainstream media will be WE NEED STRICTER GUN CONTROL.

No, we don't, stupid. What we do need is to collectively wake back up to the fact that with great power comes great responsibility. You see, despite what the media would like you to think, gun ownership in this country is a *right*, not a privilege. And the nasty little thing about rights is that they come with responsibilities. Uncle Ben knew that, and if you haven't been recently lobotomized by one of those killer metal straws they're selling now to save the world, you know it, too. The man who committed this crime should be punished to the fullest extent of the law for attempted murder. He should be stripped of his rights because he voluntarily gave them up the moment he pulled the trigger. Guns are for just about everything *but* unprovoked violence.

And if you consider a lousy haircut to be justification enough to try to give somebody a hot lead facelift, then your ass needs to be off the streets.

It's just a haircut, people—you need to calm down. Drink some of that blue liquid the barber's got; that should do the trick. ★

Area 51

Okay, I know it's all one big joke, but I can't get off this topic. Let's talk a little bit about bad ideas. One of the things that highlights the more interesting periods of development in our lives is the series of bad ideas we have—or at least the ones we act on. Buying a timeshare, eating chicken medium rare, buying one-ply toilet paper on Taco Tuesday—these are all classic examples of the bad idea, the execution of which will lead to mayhem and sorrow.

But exhibit A in the current court of public opinion has surely got to be the Area 51 raid. Now, for those of you who don't spend the entirety of your day reading through Facebook, you're welcome—I, Chad Prather, am there every day so that you don't have to be. Lurking in the shadows, fighting crime, and kissin' on people upside-down in the rain, I'm just your friendly neighborhood be-hatted crusader. I'm the hero you need, not the hero you deserve. I see nothin' but gaggles of fools doin' stupid crap all day, every day, and then I come on here to talk to you fine people about it. So imagine my complete and utter lack of surprise when I found out that a bunch of video-game-playing millennials has come up with a plan to storm Area 51, the idea being that "they can't stop us all." Folks, this is the "Moron Hunger Games." This is the Chernobyl of weekend plans. I've seen diagrams, and these goofy-ass people are mapping this thing out like they're invading Normandy, but lookin' for Pokemon on the beaches instead of Germans.

Now I'm as curious as anybody about the stuff they're hidin' at Area 51. I don't think its aliens, though. I think maybe Biggie and 'Pac are in there strategizin' on how to save the rap industry. Maybe they've got the frequently asked questions from AOC's Green New Deal in a filing cabinet somewhere. Or, if we're real lucky, there's a secret stash of Tickle Me Elmos there, and the government is just waiting for the right time to unleash them on the public. Or maybe there's a real-life laser-eyed mean greenie in there code named "Elmo" that has a hankering for human offal.

I can't stress enough how dumb of an idea storming Area 51 with a bunch of dude-bro, "weekend warcraft," croc-wearin', "I haven't bathed in three weeks," Beto lovers really is. Our military is the most powerful force in the history of the world, and they are apt to light your candy asses up if you go runnin' 'em like that. You know what a tank and a good chain-gun'll do to a bunch of idiots all tryin' to pull a Leeroy Jenkins at the same time? Wet red dust in the wind, baby.

You see, the whole problem with this idea, aside from that whole practical part where you get shot, is that you're lookin' for instant gratification. You want to know something real bad, and you want to share it with the world, and screw the consequences. But that isn't how the real world works, and it ain't ever gonna be.

So listen up, Moronials and Generation Pee-your-pantsers. You really wanna know what's in Area 51, here's what you do. Get a job! Make some money so that you can go back to school and get a degree! Then join the fine establishment that is our military and work your way up through the military intelligence community. Then, someday, maybe you'll walk up to that security checkpoint in the blazing hot Nevada desert, and instead of merking your butt on sight, they'll open up the gate and let you in. It'll be like getting a black belt in martial arts: by the time you've got the skills to kill some people, you've also got the discipline not to.

Don't raid Area 51, folks! Don't do it! If Alf is still locked up in there, let him get out his own dern self. ★

Sixteen-Year-Old Voters

So a lot of soul-sucking politicians are pushing for the voting age to be lowered to 16. You have got to be kidding me. When I was 16, I could barely figure out how to open my high school locker every day. I was in tenth grade with raging hormones and pimples, chasing girls and taking geometry for the second time. The last thing on my mind was politics. I didn't want to get out of bed much less understand the fundamentals of the Electoral College.

Nancy Pelosi says that young people are more open-minded and she's always been in favor of 16-year-olds voting. Woman you wouldn't let a 16-year-old chauffeur you around town or spit in his ear if his brain was on fire. What they need to do is change the requirements so that an Alzheimer's patient can't be Speaker of the House.

When I was 16, my car got so full of people one night that we had to make two boys ride in the trunk. We used my mother's 15 passenger van to surf on top of it because we thought we were teen wolves. I thought Poison was a good band. I thought I had found the love of my life and wore popped collars. When I was 16, my friends and I gathered up a bunch of cats and turned them loose in a local Chinese restaurant. Yes . . . of course I should've been punching ballots. Sixteen-year-olds don't pay taxes, have their own health insurance, or have dependents. They are too busy playing Fortnite and World of Warcraft on a gaming system they didn't even buy themselves. I'm not saying they're dumb, but they are dumb. I know. I was one and have had several. Any parent out there knows what I'm talking about. Ask a teacher. Not a single one of you looks at your 16-year-old and says, "Oh yeah, they should be picking the leaders of the free world."

Former Texas congressman and presidential candidate Robert Francis "Beto" O'Rourke (a 45-year-old man) was apologizing to America for the stuff he wrote when he was 16. Give me a break, dude. You do know that 16 is the age where kids look at Tide PODS and think, "Hey that looks tasty." Only low information and unintelligent people vote for a party that thinks men are women and women are men, borders are evil, socialism is good, and babies should be killed at 40 weeks of pregnancy. They fool full-grown adults with that crap by promising free stuff and claiming to be a so-called party of tolerance, so you know kids will eat that stuff up faster than Michael Moore with a box full of Dunkin' Donuts. Just a few years ago Democrats were saying that 26-year-olds needed to stay on their parents' health insurance because it was too difficult for them to navigate, but now they want them to vote. Can they buy guns, smokes, booze? Can we send them to war, Nancy? Should we let them get legally married? Should they be allowed to fly a commercial jet? How 'bout we let them run for office themselves. Come on, Nancy, don't you want to debate a 16-year-old from the twelfth congressional district of California? Seriously. Come on, bae, don't you wanna get turnt up with a woke squad of OC's throwing shade on the debate stage and thirsty for 420 and finna bust yo basic Boujie OG bubble. Don't leave me on read, Nancy. That ain't Gucci.

Let's face it: kids would vote exactly the way their parents tell them to. At the rate liberals execute their unborn, maybe I should rethink my position here. But I digress.

Can we please at least try to restore a little sanity to our world rather than letting our hunger for power and control continue to bring us downward into craziness and dumb ideas. ★

America Is
Pretty Great

L et me explain something that some of you might not like: America is pretty dang awesome. Now hear me out before you start building your big checklist of all we've ever done wrong. And we've done plenty. I wanna remind you that your granddaddy didn't give Hitler the DDT so that you could whine and apologize for being American. Where you wanna be? France? Is the Tricolor planted on the moon? Nope.

Yada yada, fill in your associated sense of victimhood here. More than 300 million people call the United States home and possess more liberty than we know what to do with. That's a lot of folks with a lot of diversity and a lot of opinions. Like fingerprints, no two are the same. It's no wonder we tend to get at each other's throats when we've forgotten that differing opinions are one of the things that built this incredible country. It's okay to be different if ultimately you can also share the same basic values and goals. Like liberty. Liberty is something we all better value above our differences. Liberty is the seedbed whereby our differences can exist and also what reminds us that we are all still cut from the same crazy bolt of cloth.

And no, I'm not giving credence to any form of extremism. That's not fundamentally American. That tends to be a minority of mouthy morons and is not in any way foundational to anything we are trying to accomplish. I'm talking about you and your neighbor. The real world you live in and not the virtual cyber world or the 24-hour news cycle that funnels man's inhumanity to man into our daily field of vision and gets us lathered up like a hillbilly who lost his moonshine still. No, America affords us the right to pursue happiness. Not many places in the world do that. Doesn't guarantee us that we'll ever find it, but it definitely reminds us that there's nothing that can stand in the way of our ambition and keep us from potentially getting it. So go get happy, America. Remember happiness? Chase it. Strive for it. Pursue it. Don't let any form of tyranny stop you from grabbing it. We don't do tyranny up in here, remember? Our forefathers knew that people need to be free and that power-hungry jacklegs would always try to steal it. So they created a system of government that guaranteed that power will consistently slip from the fingers of those who abuse it. That in and of itself ought to make you happy. It's okay to be a happy patriot today. It's okay to show it outwardly. Pursue happiness, America. Value liberty. Celebrate life. ★

The Problem
with
Washington

Hey, Washington, I know that you are all politicians, so I'm very well aware of the fact that you've grown accustomed to having words go in one ear and out the other virtually unhindered by anything resembling brain matter, but please do your best to listen up for just a brief moment. I'm an American citizen who loves his country and the ideals of the American Constitution passionately and with a great zeal. Like many Americans both past and present, I am discouraged by the lack of leadership qualities that I see among your ranks in DC. In fact, I feel that you are no longer leading at all but rather meandering in the darkness and hoping to find our future by luck or happenstance. One can only deduce by your bickering and truth twisting, your condescending attitudes toward each other, as well as the American people who put you in your historically esteemed office, that you have no idea what you're doing beyond your proverbial grandstanding, lecturing, and backbiting. Your obvious and main goal seems to be to remain in a position of power—and that at all costs. You don't care who you have to spy on, lie about, cheat with, compromise, undermine, subvert, sabotage, or swindle to do it. Now maybe that's how it's done these days in Washington, DC, in the honored halls of Congress and the Senate. Kinda reminds me of a young person who thinks that the best way to lose weight is to stick her finger down her throat every time she eats. I'm telling you there's a better way. Maybe walk across the street and read the Constitution and then remind yourself that this thing you're doing inside the beltway is about WE the people.

How dare I lecture you! How dare you create the necessity for the lecturing! Now you can puff your chest out with a self-righteous how dare you, but I'd ask you to puff it right back in and humble yourselves in the face of the American people—a people who have fought, died, and sacrificed life, limb, and long hours for you to be in your lofty seat.

It doesn't matter what the media think of you. It matters what we the people think of you.

No sir and no ma'am, most of us don't know how it "works" up there in Washington, but we do know what you told us before we cast the ballot to put you there. We know the promises you made. We'd appreciate it if you'd try to live up to your word. And yes, I know that's a foreign concept in this current age of political relativism. I'd remind you that every single one of you said something about being bipartisan and reaching across the aisle in your campaign speeches, but with how you're behaving, it seems your idea of bipartisanship is cutting one wing off the bird and wishing him Godspeed and perfect health. Don't forget to pose for the picture after you do it. You'll look good on the cover of the *New York Times.*

In short, we the people are sick of the political posturing that you are engendering. It's impotent, and you know it.

We are tired of bickering back and forth with our neighbors over ideologies we hold dear only to see you consistently, passionately, and articulately defecate on them. Maybe it's true that the governors need to be once again advised by the governed. You exist where you are today because at some point your people believed in you. Help us to believe in you again. ★

THE AOC
ECONOMIST

Ladies and gentlemen, I am positively quivering with excited reverence as I bask in the acres of shade cast by the monumental dome of Our Lady of the Woke, Alexandria Ocasio-Cortez. Yes, this Instagram heiress of the fortune that favors the boneheaded graces us with her intellect on a fairly routine basis, bringing us solutions to life's problems in the form of product reviews, Instant Pot recipes, and, most recently, a form of economic savvy that you almost have to be crazy to even begin to understand. Maybe not almost.

Last year, everyone in the wide world of the web was waxing antagonistic in the general direction of our pop-eyed political princess because she had the audacity to invent a twentieth-century economist named Milton Keynes, whom she paraphrased in an effort to back up her own substantially well-thought-out Bartenderian Economic Theory. Indeed, the brushfire of backlash grew to a white-hot flash of rage on the part of the racist, bigoted, xenophobic, and misogynistic far right, amidst the furor of which they claimed she was confusing economists Milton Friedman and John Maynard Keynes—you'll note the difference in pronunciation, because everyone else did.

Now, as you can see and have no doubt heard from all your friends, I wear a cowboy hat. Generally speaking, that lumps me in with all the knuckle-dragging, mouth-breathing, window-licking confab of conservative consciousness you've all come to know and look down upon as a sacrament of your woke sacred rituals. But today I must part from my good-intentioned but poorly educated tribe of limitless hatred to land squarely on the side of Ms Ocasio-Cortez.

I know, you're checking out the window even now to see if there are pigs flying in the sky or if perchance a surprise weather report of snow in the Underworld has popped up on TV. But hear me out.

The economics of Milton Friedman—known as *monetarist economics*—and the economics of John Maynard Keynes—known as *Keynesian economics*—are so wildly different that only a person without a pulse to pump blood to the brain could possibly confuse them. Put simply, the former approaches economics from a capitalistic perspective, surmising that the most amount of limitation possible on the government and the least amount of regulation of business will lead to the most robust economy. The latter, on the other hand, states from a socialistic perspective that the capricious nature of the markets invites a firm and steady regulatory hand on the part of the government in order to synthetically—one might say artificially—maintain economic stability.

Now I don't know about you, but I recognize in the words of Alexandria Ocasio-Cortez the genius of combining these two figures. Not only is turning two famous economists into one conjoined twin a bold move in uniting our wildly polarized American citizenry, but it also does what I like to think of as covering all the bases. In a modern world where being right and being accurate are increasingly distant kissing cousins, it's vital to be able to back up anything you ever say with a quote from someone, no matter how insanely crazy the thing you're saying is. In one swift motion, AOC has created out of two whole cloths a fictional flimflam economist who may end up being more famous than either of his two real progenitors, merely by dint of having poured forth from the too-red-lipstick font of Ocasio-Cortez's wisdom hole.

Weep for society, brothers and sisters! Or, alternatively, learn to laugh at the dipshits of the world, and try to stay sane out there. ★

The Iran-Iraq Rant

I feel like somebody just gave me a belated Christmas present, you all. In case you haven't heard yet, we had ourselves a little Benghazi-like situation at the American Embassy over in Iraq the other day. Hezbollah militia members, after killing an American citizen in a rocket attack a few days earlier, proceeded to set one of the embassy buildings on fire. And because we have a president in office whose interests don't align with your average naughty jihadi with a bomb strapped to his body, we went in and kicked some ass American-style, instead of leaving our folks in the embassy to be harassed or even killed by terrorists . . . you know, Obama- and Hillary-style. Indeed, the United States military, in its fervent devotion to the policy of Walk Softly but Carry a Big Airstrike, killed the shit out of Iran's top general—a guy who's been neck deep in terrorism for a long time. Goooooood riddance.

Now this is just the latest escalation in what's been an uneven-as-hell, bringing-a-knife-to-a-gunfight verbal hoedown of a showdown that's been going on since the seventies, when the mullahs first arrived on the proverbial scene. The government of Iran hates the state of Israel, they hate the United States, and they're the chief sponsors of terrorism in the world. Conversely, the people of Iran live in a daily nightmare of state subjugation. Before the mullahs arrived, they were happy and a helluva lot freer. They wore bell-bottomed jeans, listened to American records, and were a lot more into doing the Hustle than the Holla for Allah.

It's a damn shame, really, because if their government's not careful, they're about to find themselves in the kind of fight where we turn you into warm glass. The United States has time and time again extended a kind of mercy to the Iranian government in the form of economic and political sanctions. It's like your Daddy whipping you with a belt so that he doesn't have to shoot your butt. Yet Iran never learns, and its people are apt to pay at least some of the consequences if their leadership doesn't back down from us.

Iran, if you're watching out there—and I know you are—listen up, because I'm trying to save you. You're messing with America. We kill people in church when we have to. We're a mostly friendly grizzly bear, but you poke us at your extreme peril. And we've got a wild man at the helm of the starship—you piss us off enough, and we'll light you up like a menorah on the last day of Hanukkah . . . I think that's how that works. Take a hint: go bury whatever's left of your terrorist general, limp on back home, and go do laundry or something, because it ain't worth the fight.

The mainstream media have already begun to spin this to make it look like Trump was out of line for standing up to these Persian pains in the ass—don't buy it, people! If we end up in a real fight with Iran, it's been a long time coming, and they're going to deserve what they get. We should never hope for war or even skirmishes—but when they're upon us, we will celebrate the victory. In this case, before it's even won—because it will be won. ✶

The Colin Kaepernick Rant

The Kaep is back!

    I'm talking about the man, the myth, the legend—the dude who made big waves and eventually big bucks by availing himself of the opportunity to drop a knee right into the giant pile of horse manure that is American racial politics. Colin Kaepernick. This is the same Bob Ross–inspired dude-bro with a dude-fro who got famous not for being a good football player but for having the bravery to rise from his millionaire status and his upper-middle-class upbringing and rain down righteous verbal fire on the men and women of America's police forces by referring to them as racist pigs. Yes, this half-black, half-white and all-American imbecile walks upon the surface of the troubled racial waters like Jesus Christ himself, but instead of reaching out a hand to calm the storm, he's calling for more thunder and lightning.

    Fortunately, his execution of the cause has all the leakproof integrity of a mob-run boxing match; in the effort to rid the world of cruelty and unfairness, he has teamed up with—or perhaps chained himself to?—Nike, one of the more legendary employers of fine sweatshop labor in the world. And you've got to give the Kaep some credit: whatever sway it is that Nike thinks he has over the American public must be huge, because they listen to him. Not too long ago, Kaepernick called them up and told them that a line of shoes showing the Betsy Ross flag was racist—and Nike pulled the shoe. I about lost my damn mind when that happened—I wondered then and wonder now what flagrant sin he must have at some point walked in on at Nike headquarters to garner such power, especially when you consider that, as of the moment, he's not a football player, just some kind of weird AstroTurf lawn gnome.

We all watched with amusement a few weeks back when Kaepernick pulled the ultimate arrogant move and didn't show up to the NFL workout he had scheduled and instead decided to hold his own workout elsewhere, as if that's how it works. Shoot, at this point the NFL would rather sign Uncle Rico on and listen to him talk about throwing the football over a mountain than deal with this spoiled brat.

And yet . . .

And yet here's Nike, still somehow finding a way to capitalize on this albatross hanging about the NFL's neck. A couple weeks ago they launched a line of Kaepernick-inspired shoes, which sold out in minutes online. Minutes, folks! What the hell is going on around here? For a little over a hundred bucks—which is about what the Kaep's football career is worth these days—you can be the proud owner of a pair of Nike-endorsed reminders that you should hate all police for the crimes—and in some cases supposed crimes—of a few. Who's buying these things? I think it's Kaepernick himself, and he's just got a closet at home full of shoes and hairspray cans.

From the very beginning, this whole thing has seemed like a ploy on Kaepernick's part to first become, and then stay, relevant. But the unfortunate side effect is that he stands for something that is both disgusting and dangerous to the tattered fabric of our society. Obviously, black lives matter, Kaep. But when you go about talking about it the way you do and then sell yourself out to some of the last people who should be talking about public injustice, you're a little hard to take seriously.

And one more thing: I saw a picture of Kaepernick recently, and it was on Facebook, so it must be real. It shows the Kaep flashing the—wait for it—okay hand sign at the camera. Shock and awe, folks! My determination is that Colin's white half is trying to oppress his black half—thank God he's got that Chia Pet on his head to protect the side that's supposed to win.

Don't be like Kaepernick, folks. Go out there and live your lives, and let others live theirs. And stand up for justice when you can; just make sure your stand isn't a super obvious bid for fame and fortune. ★

The Tulsi Gabbard Rant

Tulsi Gabbard—let's talk about her for a minute. As plenty of you probably know, Tulsi came out on the Twitters the other day and gave a Christmas greeting that was so warm and sincere—and so devoid of the standard intersectional tripe to which we've become accustomed these days—I had to do a double take and make sure I was looking at a real Democrat, and I almost spilled my pregame Boxing Day beer. But there she was, talking not only about Christmas as being the time of the year in which we celebrate Jesus's birth but also the time of year when we most recognize the thing that Jesus stood for: serving God and serving others.

Now this is just one of several things that Tulsi has done lately that I'm fond of—a couple of weeks ago, she voted "present" during the impeachment hearing for Donald Trump, which was a ballsy move for a person running for president on the Democratic ticket. She clarified later that while she thinks Donald Trump is unfit for the office of the president, she didn't feel like the proceedings in question were honest and transparent and thus couldn't vote for impeachment. Seems like this particular Democrat may have caught herself a nasty case of integrity. To top it all off, Hillary Clinton said she's a Russian asset, which makes her practically a saint in my book. And I know, I know, between those of you out there who'd love to see her come over to the Republican Party and those of you who just think she's hot, she's apt to either get red-pilled or red-rocketed, but hold up.

Slow your roll and let the Political Cowboy bend your ear a little.

Here's the potential problem with Tulsi. It's unlikely but possible that when the time comes for her Democratic candidacy to do the air dance, she's going to come back as an independent and try to defeat Donald Trump. And while that might seem like a perfectly normal thing to do, it could be bad for us if she ends up being a spoiler. In case you all don't remember, the late Ross Perot—another politician of moral character who ran outside the Republican circle—ran in previous elections and arguably got Bill Clinton elected twice as a result. And while I admire Tulsi Gabbard's pluck and seeming integrity as a political candidate, I don't much care for the idea that she might upset the apple cart in 2020. It's not like I'm going to vote for her, and it's probably not like you are either. But there are enough people in this country who exist in the ideological middle and who are mighty tired of the tribalist two-tone terror that has been the American political system for years now. These are the people who are most likely to look at the acrimonious ass-hattery of the current bevy of Democrats, stack it up against the booming Trump economy, and lean right, lean right, even during the lean-left part of the song. I'm not saying the 2020 election counts on that happening, necessarily, but it could.

Now Tulsi, if you're listening—and I'm assuming you are—here's the thing: I like you. And what's more, I respect you. You've served your country in the U.S. military, and you're a credit to your party, even if that's saying next to nothing. I get why you don't want Trump to be in office, but if you genuinely value truth, freedom, and the American way, don't do anything that's apt to result in us having to deal with one of these socialist window-lickers for the next four years. You're better than that. ★

The Impeachment Rant

Holy ineffectual political strategy, Batman! The Democratic Party finally went and did what they've been wanting to do since the day Donald Trump swung onto the scene on a long-ass red tie. I'm talking impeachment, baby! That's right, the totally nonpartisan, unbiased, pure-as-the-driven-snow Honest Johns of the House Democrats have shot their figurative wad on the off chance that the Senate Republicans are all going to do a Jim Jones move on their political careers and oust the president. Well, I wouldn't mix up the Flavor-Aid just yet, because what's almost certainly going to happen on the Senate side of this is a big fat nothing.

And yet, mainstream and social media exploded moments after the announcement of the impeachment, and a ton of people on the left were wetting their pants in joy, blissfully unaware that an impeachment in the House does not a removal make.

You see, for the uninitiated, here's how this works. The House of Representatives gets to charge the president with a set of crimes—or in this case, they get to charge him with a crime full of holes so big you could drive a Prius through it and another crime so crimey it's not a damn crime. What they don't get to do is actually convict. That job falls to the Senate, which you may recall is currently under Republican control. Old Turtlehead Mitch McConnell and his gaggle of senatorial sharecroppers are not only going to drop this whole thing, but they're also going to spend the next year making enough political hay to withstand the Storm of 2020! I'll be honest, I got a little aroused just then.

At any rate, this puts me—and I'd imagine a lot of you—in a very interesting place, historically speaking. Come November of this next year, I will be voting for an impeached president, which is something I'd never even considered before. I've thought of voting for a few dead ones, but never an impeached one. And honestly, I can't think of a cooler thing in the eventual annals of history than to have been on the side of right. Someday, when those history books and the media that write them catch up to the truth, they're all going to look back on this time as a seminal moment in America's history; we've been turning the ship around for three years now, and by wrongfully impeaching the president, I suspect the Democrats have all but guaranteed that we're going to get another four in the next election.

I like that Trump's a wrecking ball. I like that he's brash and breaks stuff. And I like the things I'm seeing restored in my country. Thanks for what you're doing, Mr. President, and don't worry—we'll still respect you in the morning. ★

Greta Thunberg Rant

What in the Swedish-fish-choking-on-plastic is going on around here?! Greta Thunberg is not only back in the news where she doesn't belong, but she has been declared *Time Magazine*'s Person of the Year. That's right, the winner of 2019's illustrious POTY award goes to the temperamental teenager with a touch of the 'tism. You know, the girl who could have been passionate about algebra and saying things like "How square you?" and nobody would've known who she is—but who happens to be passionate about climate change and is therefore more famous than God right now.

Now I think its time we had a little heart-to-heart about Greta. I know we all like to poke fun, and we're justified in it. Leave aside for a second the steaming pile of crap that's poured over us conservatives' heads every day by the liberal media—sometimes things are just funny—and just about everything surrounding Greta Thunberg falls into that category. But here's the deal: I, like most of you, know where to draw the line when it comes to mockery. But hooboy, there are some of you out there who need to get some more Jesus into your lives. You know who you are.

Listen up, hayseed: while you're out there trolling the Yuletide away, slugging back shots of Kentucky Deluxe and field stripping your pack of Marlboros in three and a half seconds, the rest of us are left to clean up the mess in your wake. Don't get me wrong; Greta's got the same kind of fingernails-making-love-to-a-chalk-board vocal qualities as an Elizabeth Warren or a Kamala Harris, and the bullshit that falls out of her piehole is thick enough and deep enough to grow a whole new crop of CO_2-eating trees. But she's also a kid. And as I've said before, kids are stupid—it isn't their fault; God made them that way so that we could control them long enough to get them out of the house safely.

And what's worse is this: she's not happy. And I mean really not happy. She's said that before getting involved in protesting climate change, she was directionless, not interested in anything . . . in short, she was downright depressed. Well now, what do you think is going to happen to Greta when one of these days she grows up and finds out that the apocalyptic end of her childhood was more the result of poor decisions on the part of her parents than anything climate change could've ever done? Talk about depression; hell, her pigtail already looks like she's practicing how to tie a noose.

Now, as you know perfectly well, I don't have any problem whatsoever with calling out nonsense when I see it. And I don't have any problem with poking fun at people—I'm spending at least half an hour a day working on my Swedish accent just in case Greta ends up running for Congress someday. But I do think it behooves us to realize that in some cases the subject of our ire deserves a little pity thrown in with the pithy. We can be brash without being bullies. Remember, the ultimate goal we should have with someone like Greta is for her to come to the kind of Damascus Road realization of the error of her ways so that she can be one of the more powerful advocates against this kind of corrupt, catastrophist thinking. People can change—it does happen. ★

Pushing God Out of Culture—or—Atheist, Meet Thy Foxhole

I n his stunning work of philosophical genius, *Also Sprach Zarathustra*, Friedrich Nietzsche lamented (or celebrated, if you're reading it through pink-lensed leftist glasses) that "God is dead." Furthermore, man was the one who killed Him. Now I don't always take my philosophy from a man with a mustache the size of a snowplow, but in Nietzsche's case, I tend to think his observation was salient, to say the least. Obviously, man did not literally kill God—the closest we've ever come to that was when Morgan Freeman was in an automobile accident a while back.

But in terms of the development of our society at large—and increasingly on an individual level as well—it does seem that in the past century or two God has pretty much gotten the boot. And in case you're wondering, I do actually mostly just mean the God worshipped in Christianity. Allah, despite pretty regularly taking a whiz on the couch and bumping into people with a lamp-shade on his head, has as yet not been disinvited from the party.

Now I'm a hopeless sentimental type, but even I'm not sappy enough to be of the opinion that when this country was founded, everyone in America was some pure-as-the-driven-snow pur-veyor of puritanical perfection upon the populace. I don't buy into the notion that when the free love generation came about, we collectively dove headfirst down the mineshaft leading to Hell. But I will say that in the process of throwing the baby Jesus out with the holy water, we've made it easier and easier over time for the values we did share as a country to begin to erode.

And if you let something fall away long enough, eventually there's nothing left. This is why I use Just for Men.

So what values, exactly, am I talking about? What is it about having God in our midst that's so necessary? I'll explain; let me just take my vagina hat off and put my cowboy hat back on.

You see, ideologically America is like one of those merry-go-rounds we used to be able to play on when we were kids (I have no idea if they're still around, but they seem like the type of thing leftists would call dangerous, mostly because they're fun). The solid center of American values is the notion of individual liber-ty—I get a bit of a chubby just thinking about it—and it's the most sacred of the traditions we hold, both inside and outside of our faiths. Those of us who cling to it understand that it's a wild ride: when that thing's spinning around, you've got to hold tight to the bars, tuck in your legs, and remember that barf follows the rules of centrifugal force.

The phrase "freedom isn't free" doesn't just mean that people have to lay their lives down for it—though it means that, too. It also means that the natural tendency of mankind when we form societies is to eventually break them apart—because when you get down to it, we're dumb as rocks. Apathy and stupidity are, nine times out of ten, the great destroyer of worlds.

America is unique in the world for its approach to this, and the grand experiment that we've been running all these years has been and always will be just that, an experiment. We're experimenting to see if we can keep it going.

Removing God from our paradigm is problematic (there, I can use that word too) because in the absence of a kind of collective blanket of faith (a place where not everyone has to have the same beliefs but where we all can agree on the ones that spring out of the pursuit of individual liberty), nihilism begins to set in. And I'm telling you, that stuff will rot your teeth out of your head. Some of the most confusing people I meet in life are what I call *cheerful nihilists.* They believe in nothing, and they want to shout it from the rooftops. And while I think most of these mop-topped bozos trying to nail moral philosophy to an ersatz cross of cotton candy are instead tenderizing their own thumbs, I have to marvel at their ability to propagate the kind of indifference that has killed a hundred million people in the past century.

When the bottom falls out, in other words, everything on top of it goes, too. We removed God from our schools, from our lives—hell, in some cases even from our churches. You ever see a Unitarian church service? It's like the worst TED Talk ever had a love child with a hair-dyeing convention. The bottom line is that without the central notion of God—whether you personally believe in Him or not—our society's great mission of maintaining personal freedom becomes more and more impossible to uphold because where there is nihilism, there is no room for genuine idealism toward that common goal. What's that old saying? If you believe in nothing, you'll fall for anything?

Maybe I should've started with that. ★

Beto Monologue

So, Robert Francis O'Rourke—in a fit of holy inspiration during the most recent Democratic debate—set down his plate of huevos rancheros; removed his sombrero, poncho, and pointy cowboy boots; and ironically ceased firing his pistola wildly in the air long enough to make a declaration to the American people that "Hell yes, we're going to take your AR-15, your AK-47!" Now, if you're like me, you had already gone out earlier in the day and purchased a comically large set of googly eyes so that you could glue them to your eyelids and pretend to be surprised at all times when stuff like this was getting said up on that stage—when, in reality, none of it surprised you. For years, we've said that Democrats are trying to destroy the Second Amendment—that they're going to try to take our guns if we don't stop them. And the response on the left has always been that we're overreacting, that they only want "commonsense" legislation, that it's never going to go too far.

It's all bullshit, folks. You're going to have to wake up to the reality of the situation, and the reality of the situation is this: ideologies are complex, and they rely on interdependent strategies to implement. I'm not talking about a conspiracy theory per se; I'm more talking about a form of mass hypnosis in the slinking form of socialism. For years, socialism has crept in, inch by inch, into our political lives and into the collective consciousness of the American people at large. You see, it kept its head low and thus was able to get past all but the most observant of people as it slowly began poisoning the well of American thought and discourse. It entrenched itself in the halls of power so well masked that up until recently you could point a finger at it and say, "That's socialism!" and all you'd get would be a retributive stare from the folks on the left and an assurance that we all love our country equally and that there's no socialism to be seen here. Move along, folks.

Bit by bit, it has gnawed at the constitutional bones upon which the framework of our great country hangs, sucking out the marrow of our enthusiasm and the lifeblood of our basic goodness. Our body politic has grown sick, weak from attack, and seemingly on the verge of collapse; a high wind at the head and a precipitously placed stone at the feet might be all it takes to topple our nation. We've acceded to the greatest heights of nobility and reward of any country in the history of the world—imagine how far we will fall if it comes to that.

Beto O'Rourke is a jackass. He's a two-bit "punkitician" whose only real reading skills seem to emerge in roomfuls of stupid people who are eager to lap up a specific variety of nonsense. Like many before him, he speaks with an obviously unearned gravitas—like a publicly disgraced charlatan giving a stilted rendering of "Sinners in the Hands of an Angry God" from the political pulpit. He lives a life of armpit stains and bad Mexican accents.

But buffoon or not, he speaks a truth of intention. Any socialist worth his salt mine knows instinctively—and probably only instinctively in most cases—that the institution of socialism doesn't mix with the retention of freedom, especially the freedom to more handily fight the institution should it rear its ugly head. Beto isn't going to be the next president, thank God. He's most likely going to just be another candidate we all shout at, then forget six months after the election because there's so damn many of them on either side each time around. But his ideas aren't going anywhere. The unmasking of socialist tactics—such as nakedly admitting that "Hell yes, we're coming for your (guns)"—is just the next step in the process. Because right now there are more guns in this beautiful country of ours than there are people, and more are being manufactured every day. Right now they can't come for our guns, no matter what Farley O'Mexican wants us to think. But it might not always be that way. And when we've reached a point where the hoods can come off and these people can flat-out state their real intentions, aren't we a little closer to the fire than you'd like to be? I know it's getting a little hot for my liking.

This next presidential election is important, possibly the most important of our lives so far. Not for Donald Trump's legacy, and not because every Democratic candidate who has a snowball's chance in hell of winning also happens to be completely insane. It's important because we need more time to stamp at the evil of socialism that's infected so much of our country at this point. You're never going to stamp it all out—man exists in a state of imperfection, and socialism is a natural outgrowth of that—but it might be possible to drive it out enough that we have a chance to rebuild the opposing ideology. You know, the one that made us great in the first place. If we get that chance, let's not waste it. There's work to be done, and you and I are the ones who are going to have to do it. We can't let our country fall to the likes of hapless socialist boobs like Beto O'Rourke; we can't let freedoms like the right we share to keep and bear arms just slip away into the ether. We've got to stand for our values. The light shines brightly into the darkness, and it overcomes the darkness. But we have to be brave enough to hold the lamp up. ★

Never Again

I want you to consider, for a moment, two seemingly disparate ideas. I want you to take the journey with me through the soggy mire of critical thinking that so often leads us to a deeper truth about life than whatever subject started us thinking in the first place. And I want you to help me try to merge these two ideas. Let's turn them into something that makes sense—because they're both true.

Alexandria Ocasio-Cortez is a woman with a household name. She is known for her bold statements about problems with our political system on everything from climate change to immigration and for solutions that tend to be—at best—problematic and empty of any real merit. Almost every time she opens her mouth on her Instagram videos or speaks in front of Congress, or even just tweets, she says something that defies you as the receiver of her wisdom to make even a shred of sense out of it. She is a former bartender who seems to have gotten caught up in the whirlwind of politics and has sunk in so far over her own head at this point that it's all she can do just to breathe. And yet . . .

And yet, among the Democrats and the mainstream media, she carries a wallet full of unearned intellectual currency. The left, in all its perspicacity and wisdom, has conflated having a spirited personality with having a firm grasp on reality. The phenomenon of the double down has reached such epic proportions in the Democratic Party at this point that if this were a real game of poker, they'd have to be betting with other people's chips by now—although let's not forget that is what they're most comfortable doing anyway.

A few months ago, Congresswoman Ocasio-Cortez stated in an Instagram video that the detention facilities down on our southern border function like—and indeed are—concentration camps. After which she stated that "'never again' means something." And of course the world of public discourse lit up into a massive inferno over this. Because the term *concentration camp* and the statement "never again" bring up one thing and one thing only in the minds of those who have even a shred of historical knowledge—and that thing is the Holocaust. There's no equivocating here, no bandying our words about to try to find a different meaning. Several people over the past few days have sought to do that, and frankly, it just makes me tired. She said what she said, people—and it means what it means. The real wonder is less that Ocasio-Cortez used the words *concentration camp* and *never again* and more that she knew them in the first place.

And why bring this up now, when the deed is long done and buried a thousand leagues beneath the roiling turmoil of an eternally fitful series of news cycles? Because despite all the screaming on both sides when this story was still young and fresh, most of the people I heard weren't really saying much. We're all so tired from the endless litany of wrongs committed against one another that we rarely stick around to untangle them to their individual roots. Personally, I like a good cooldown period in which to reflect on something and really think it through. And thus we arrive at the still-sharp horns of my dilemma.

So here are those two seemingly disparate ideas I was talking about earlier. And remember that both of these are true, so it's our job to find a way to make them work together and be part of the same reality.

On the one hand, you can look at what Ocasio-Cortez said and conclude that this is an ignorant woman saying ignorant things on a subject about which she barely has any understanding at all. The detention facilities at our southern border not only aren't anything even remotely like the concentration camps in Hitler's regime during the Second World War, but in fact what little resemblance they do bear comes directly as a result of the fact that the Democrats in Congress refuse to provide ICE with the funding it needs to fully stock these facilities. Concentration camps, as we all understand them, did not exist to facilitate the processing of refugees into a country, nor the deportation of illegal immigrants out of it. They existed to destroy a people from the ground up so that civilization would at some point turn around and say, "Where did all the Jews go? They were right here a moment ago." So, you can see, the esteemed congresswoman from New York is just exercising her right to free speech to say dumb things. And most Americans are smart enough to see through the nonsensical part of what she's saying, right? I mean, if not a majority, at least a plurality of us know what "never again" means, right? Maybe. But either way, people say stupid things all the time, and everyone knows that, to misquote *Casablanca*, the deeper thoughts and musings of any given politician don't amount to a hill of beans. It's chaff in the wind—here today and gone tomorrow.

Here's the second idea, though. What if it's all important? What if things like this are so important that the support beams of our future may crumble beneath us as a result? Ocasio-Cortez isn't just some silly bartender-turned-politician; she's a new voice of the Democratic Party, a party that slides with an exponentially increasing speed down the path toward ultimate radicalism every day. If you've spent much time in the arena of debates, you're familiar with the idea of the *slippery-slope fallacy*. It's a problem in logic wherein the person making a statement asserts that because one step has been taken, a specific series of events—usually bad ones—is likely to occur. What makes it a fallacy is that there is little to no evidence to support the series of claims, and it's important to grasp firm to that last part. Because the slippery-slope idea isn't a fallacy if what's being predicted has happened before. It's no coincidence that Alexandria Ocasio-Cortez is a democratic socialist, seeking with all her might to drag the United States into the realm that she inhabits at least theoretically. First they come for the language. Not even the language you speak, but the language that you think. To bring about the kind of change that socialists want to bring about, they have to mold minds to think in different—and much simpler—patterns than what they currently do, for the sake of pliability. It's not enough to revile Hitler and the Nazis and have that set as a fixture in your mind. Because some day, it might be convenient for the socialist types to espouse some of the same views Hitler had, and in a case like that, it would be good to have so utterly destroyed the demarcation between the desperate reality of the Nazi regime and sane life that no one can really tell the difference anymore.

The moral equivocation—the leveling of the playing field wherein Nazi concentration camps and the detention facilities at our southern border can be easily swapped out—that is a dangerous, dangerous philosophy. Countless millions of people throughout the twentieth century lost their lives because good and intelligent people allowed the moral and intellectual underpinnings of their societies to be rotted out from within by the very same kind of nonsense that Alexandria Ocasio-Cortez is peddling today.

So what's the final analysis? How do we square the fact that she has as much right to speak nonsense as any of the rest of us with the equally important fact that she is contributing to the kind of rhetorical feedback loop that might well be our downfall as a society?

I think we let her have her say, and we continue to fight bad rhetoric with good rhetoric. We fight bad faith with good faith, hateful nonsense with compassion and logic. Listen, there is a contingent of people who are going to believe anything that Alexandria Ocasio-Cortez says no matter what it is, no matter what you say to them. In the worldview held by some, she is a thought leader and—more disturbingly—a kind of spiritual leader, and neither you nor I will ever reach those people. But what about those around you every day who don't fall into that category? What about the person who reads these things on Twitter, or sees them on Instagram, or hears about them on the news and just doesn't know what to think about them? What about that person in your life who wants or maybe even needs someone to have conversations with them about the way things are, conversations filled not with tribalism and rage but with logic and decency? I think the answer to all of this is that when Alexandria Ocasio-Cortez steps up to be a thought leader, you and I need to step up and be thought leaders too. And we need to let our light shine one or two candles brighter than hers. It shouldn't be that hard to do.

Let's make a stand for decency and logic, and let's tell the Ocasio-Cortezes of the world that we refuse the narrative. We refuse to simply accept the idea that you can mow over history like grass so that every blade reaches the same height. That isn't how reality works, it isn't how history works, and it's not going to be how you work. ★

What's on My Mind

Y'all know me by now as the guy who says what's on his mind, whether it's politically correct or not, but who's got love for everybody out there and doesn't wish anybody any harm. Well, today we're gonna take a slight detour from the whole "Gandhi of Gab" approach and talk a little bit about ass-whoopins—who's been handin' 'em and who needs 'em.

See, the political conversation at large in vibrant swaths of urban acreage in this country has become so toxic of late that it has bred in the pool of shared rhetoric a dangerous, violent animus between and among what might otherwise be sane and rational people. The very foundational notion that we as a people who possess freedom of speech and ideas can and should disagree with each other peacefully so as to continue to build that more perfect union is not only eroding in these areas but is being actively dug out by fools with little toy shovels.

Take the example of Portland, Oregon, one of the bigger and brighter dumpster fires in America today. A couple of weeks ago, members of the delightful group known as Antifa decided that it would be a great idea to punch the crap out of a journalist named Andy Ngo, after which they threw milkshakes at him, shot him with silly string, and cussed him up a blue streak. Now we're talking about a guy who's maybe a hundred pounds soaking wet and who's shorter than Bernie Sanders's list of good ideas. And these people felt the need to kick his ass and scream at him.

So this antifascist group of people who act suspiciously and ironically like fascists is comprised of mask-wearing, basement-dwelling, video game–playing, deodorant-refusing, MSNBC-watching, mama bringin' 'em dinner 'cause they can't even make mac and cheese spoiled brats! When these bridge trolls minus the charm aren't busy living under squatter's rights on the internet, they're taking to the streets like methed-up white trash superheroes and delivering social justice with baseball bats and bike locks. The overwhelming majority of these deadbeat doofuses don't have the upper body strength necessary to bench press a box of Wheat Thins, but anybody's gonna crumple if ya pop 'em in the nuts with a Louisville Slugger. And you know what chaps my hide the most? They wear masks; like the little whiny cowardly bullies they are, they take care to make sure that you can't identify them. Why? Because they aren't actually standing up for something they believe in. If that were the case, I could at least respect them a little bit, even if I didn't agree with them. But no—what they're actually doing is participating in a social game, one in which everyone but the victim gets a participation trophy at the end in the form of a self-righteous sense of accomplishment and bragging rights for the next time they all meet up to drink lattes and paint "Die Trump" on each other's toenails.

Tell you what, Antifa, next time you decide you want to beat up on a conservative, why don't you fly your happy asses down here to Texas, and we'll show you whole new places you can put that bike lock sideways. We got creative ways of beatin' ass down here, too, and you're gonna love 'em. Or, better yet, why don't you grow the hell up, move out of your parents' basement, get a damn job, and finally absorb the most basic lesson when it comes to free speech: it's free for everybody.

Folks, let's get rid of this asinine notion that reckless and silly violence is the solution to all the disagreements we have as a people. There's too much progress to be made and too much freedom to enjoy and spread around for us to be pulling nonsense like this. I love y'all, even you Antifa types . . . (lean in, smile) but seriously, I'll kick ya ass. ★

Problem Solver

Folks, if there's one thing y'all know about me, it's that I'm a problem solver. Sure, I come on here to get a laugh or two, and sure, I might get distracted from the main issue by something that amuses me . . . but on the whole, I'm here to provide the world with solutions for its problems. And today I'm gonna tell you how we can solve two problems for the price of one!

The mainstream media landscape is currently littered with the burning refuse of the back-and-forth going on about reparations for slavery. You know, that thing that ended a hundred and fifty years ago? The latest landmine on which Democrats and presidential hopefuls in particular are being asked to stomp is this idea that because Black people used to be slaves generations ago, it behooves us as a country now to pay reparations to their descendants, none of whom are or ever have been slaves. Now this might seem like a no-brainer—meaning that the people who are proposing it have no brain—but the truth of the matter is that the waters are muddy in places, and this is sometimes one of them.

Is it true that none of the Black people who were enslaved before the Emancipation Proclamation and the end of the Civil War in the United States are still alive? Yes. Is it also true that none of the people who enslaved said Black folks during that time are still alive? Also yes. Is it true that there are a lot of factors that contribute to the wealth gap in America? You're pickin' up on the pattern. But to be fair, there are some considerations on the other side. Jim Crow laws in the South did a lot of damage to Black folks for decades, and some of those people are still alive today. And I wouldn't even deny that there's a slight ripple effect that can still be felt in some places, although it gets weaker with every passing year.

Ultimately, though, reparations in our modern world are a bad idea because what do they look like? Uncle Sam's gonna take a bunch of money out of my pocket—when I didn't do anything wrong—and give it to Jerome over here—when he didn't have anything wrong done to him? How is that fair? In a hundred and fifty years is Jerome's descendant gonna have to shell out some coin to pay my descendant because the government unfairly fleeced my sorry ass? Ya never know; it could happen. Folks, one of the most important things we can remember in our day-to-day lives is that there is a massive difference between the genuine kindheartedness and fairness shown by individuals and groups of individuals and the faceless so-called justice generally promulgated by the government. The former is good; the latter is dangerous.

So what's this grand solution you've been talkin' up, Chad? People on the go are in the need to know. Just calm down there, Buzz Saw, and let Chad spoon-feed you the answer at his own pace. I say we need a bold, beautiful, and absolutely balls-to-the-wall crazy answer, and it's this:

You want to pay reparations to the people who were affected by slavery? You're gonna need a time machine. That's right, the United States government needs to invent a time machine. "But Chad!" you say. "That's impossible!" (waving your hands dismissively). Don't talk to me about impossible. If there's one group of people on this Earth who are gifted beyond measure at attempting impossible things, it's our government. And remember when I said that I was going to solve two problems with one solution? I haven't forgotten the sweet, sweet second part. Who's gonna head up the committee to get this time machine built? Damn right, AOC—Alexandria Ocasio-Cortez. In fact, not only is she going to lead the charge to build the first-ever time machine in mankind's history, but she's also gonna be the representative of our time to the freed slaves from the days of yore. Think of it! We'll send her back to deliver the reparations directly, face to face. (Pause) And if we forget to put a return button on the time machine? Oh well . . .

Take care of each other—not because the government tells you to but because you choose to, keep an eye on your wallet any time a Democrat walks by, and have a great day. ★

Censorship

olks, I want you to imagine for a moment—if you will—that you're sitting in a pottery class. And you're about to take that big old hunk of clay that's sitting in front of you, and you're going to turn it into a masterpiece. Now this ain't your first rodeo; you've got your bowl of water for the clay, your potter's wheel, and your ugly-ass curtain of an artist's smock on. "Unchained Melody" is on the record player, and Patrick Swayze's ghost is feelin' ya up from behind, all the while prayin' he don't have to possess the body of Whoopi Goldberg later. Just as you get that pottery wheel spinning, though, someone bursts through the door waving a badge and shouting for you to stop what you're doing. "You gotta know the rules," says this charter member of the ceramic constabulary. "You can spin that clay on the wheel all day long if you feel like it, but you're not allowed to use your hands to shape it anymore." (Pause) Welcome to being up shit creek without a paddle, folks. What are you supposed to do, leave that clay spinning on the wheel, looking like shaved lamb in a Mediterranean restaurant all day? No. But without the ability to use your hands, you can't shape it into the thing it wanted to be. And don't tell me you're gonna use your feet. Ugh. Y'all are just nasty.

This notion is similar to the ideological contention that you should not and therefore cannot use your words as tools to give form to shapeless substance in our public discourse, a notion that sadly gains traction over and over again throughout the course of history—and it's alive and well today, brothers and sisters! The battle we fight against censorship is probably as old as civilization itself and probably just as dumb as it ever was. For instance, recently people have been talking about changing the dictionary definition of the word *black* because the current definition—in its fullness—contains things that are derogatory to Black people. (Exasperated sigh.) Now look here: the closest thing I've ever seen to a human being actually *looking* black was Jimmy Kimmel . . . but we'd best not get into that, I expect. But there are seriously folks out there who believe that if we just change the definition of a word that encompasses so much more in the world than just the mislabeled tone of one's skin, we'll be one step closer to that final utopia we're all searching for. What's that look like, you ask? I dunno. Maybe it looks like Black people sitting on the porch sippin' on a mint julep while white people pick cotton in the fields and whip themselves. That seems to be about the pace they're going for.

Now I know . . . y'all are thinking that this is just fun and games. Sure, these people mean what they're saying, but they don't really have the power to change the meaning of words; and even if they did, so what? It's not like that changes much in the bigger picture.

It changes the mentality, folks. It shifts our paradigm from an existence wherein we are responsible to police ourselves in polite society to the degree we see fit to one wherein someone else has the authority to come in and tell you how to do it, and you just accept it because you don't think there's any other way. You've been programmed to think that. It's the difference between freedom and slavery, in all honesty.

We're living in a world now where people's careers are being brought down by the very social media that helped create them.

Why? Censorship. Facebook and Twitter don't like what you have to say? Why they'll just demonetize you and maybe squeeze your viewership numbers so hard they'll be squeaking out "Ave Maria" in a high falsetto. Listen up, Magic Shoes: is it their right as a private company to do that? Maybe. But if so, we'd better start lookin' elsewhere in the world to get our social media jollies on because these platforms have a lot of fingers in a lot of pies. They're already influencing the way our society works and the legislation that drives it—whether legal or not, their censorship of conservative voices is real, and it's real wrong. Get out there and dig them fingers into that clay. Don't let today's so-called moral authority—these sheep in wolves' clothing—stop you from using your words however you damn well please. Remember that words are tools, but they're also the window through which the light of your mind can shine out to the world. And whatever you do, keep your head on a swivel because that ghost of Patrick Swayze can get mighty handsy. ★

Saudi Arabia

Are y'all kidding me? So it turns out that the United States may end up using a loophole to sell weapons to our good, gentle, warmhearted friends over in Saudi Arabia. Now if you've never taken the time to grab a picnic blanket off the head of some Saudi prince, spread it out over the sand with a nice basket of falafel and French fries, and spend a day or two luxuriating in their society, let me clue you in on a couple of things you might not be aware of. First and foremost, this ally of convenience is a precivilized peninsula overrun by billionaire bullies who desperately want to keep alive the dream of living in the modern material world without having to shoulder any of the responsibility that comes with actually being modern! The government of Saudi Arabia is a walking human civil rights violation—complete with torturous punishment of its citizens, executions in the form of public beheadings right and left, and an attitude toward women and women's rights so heinous that I'm surprised Alyssa Milano hasn't flown over there in an F-16 to bring some feminist justice.

And yet, through all of this, Saudi Arabia remains not merely a country with whom we are neutral—at least that could possibly make some sense—but rather a country with whom we are allied! Recently, President Trump has been making an effort to get a weapons sale worth billion and billions of dollars passed through Congress. And he's trying to do it by declaring an emergency as a kind of loophole. Don't know what any of this means? Well listen up, ShortBread, and let me tell ya.

You see, the idea is that Saudi Arabia, and a bunch of other countries in the region, are mostly worried about having to deal with Iran. Now that makes sense—Iran is another one of those countries whose main goal seems to be dousing the civilized world in gasoline and then lighting a fart in its general direction. Iran and Saudi Arabia hate each other and have for years, and it stands to reason that if the Saudis don't arm themselves pretty heavily, they could be looking at an Iranian invasion force one of these days. After all, it stands to reason that the Iranians want the same thing out of the Saudis that we do—that sweet, sweet crude oil we've all heard about so much.

Folks, it's not news to you that we've been allied with Saudi Arabia for years because of their oil reserves. It's also not news to you that we've chained ourselves to some really bad people. If the brutal murder of journalist Jamal Khashoggi wasn't enough to clue you in, the ridiculous treatment of women and the bass-ackward view of the worth of human life and rights in general ought to do the trick. I'm not saying that Iran isn't a danger to the region and, in some senses, even to the world—it is. But we have to be careful who we're allying ourselves with. The evil that they do will reflect poorly on us, and we don't want any more tarnish on the reputation of this nation than necessary. Finally, Congress needs to grow a set and actually deal with matters like this. Otherwise, that's how we get undeclared wars. And I think you all know how that tends to turn out. ★

Bye Bye Miss American Lie— or—Blaze, OAN, and Newsmax Oh My!

Y'all out there in the wonderful wide world of social media—living your lives and going to your jobs and raising your youngins, and maybe hoppin' onto this page and others like it every now and then for a laugh and a few interesting thoughts—well, I've got good news and bad news for you. The good news is that we're getting rid of the bad news. It's slow, but it's coming. All of you out there who get tired of the daily heaping helping of fearmongering, race-baiting tribalistic prevarications spewing forth from the last holdouts of a species that can only exist within the confines of its own echo chamber— things are about to change. You see, the mainstream media as we have come to see them in today's world are like a prize stallion. He used to be bold and beautiful, barreling down the racetrack like thunder on hooves, but eventually he got old. He got fat and bloated and real damn gassy. He slowed down and didn't want to leave the confines of his small pasture anymore—the only thing he races to nowadays is conclusions.

And he's a lot of work to keep up with, folks. Used to be we shaped the very world we lived in based largely on what came straight from the horse's mouth. Now we're so busy trying to shovel what comes out of the other end into manageable piles that we don't have time to even think about going back to the races.

You know what they do to horses who break a leg, right? Folks, this horse breaks his leg every other week or so. Now if, like me, you cried at the end of *Old Yeller*, don't worry, this horse is euthanizing itself. You see, quite a while back it developed a pretty serious thinking problem, and it's way too late at this point for an intervention—clickbait don't wash off, as they say. Ratings are dropping, and people all over the country—hell, all over the world—are waking up to the fact that the mainstream media are basically over—and done bun can't be undone, hon.

The mainstream media had their chance to reform, in other words. In fact, they've had a lot of chances over the decades. And don't get me wrong—we Americans like ourselves a heaping plate of crap from time to time just as much as the next guy. Just ask anyone who watches "Real Desperate Housewives," assuming you can get their eyes to unglazed for a moment and they pay any attention to you when you're talking. For years now, we've even liked being fed crap in our news, but it's only because we didn't know any better. Americans are waking up to the fact that there's a new, fresh prize horse in the stall. That horse is long form, respectful, and educated conversation, and it's taking place all over the podcast world and spilling into the social media landscape on places like YouTube and Facebook. Folks like the members of the Intellectual Dark Web—groups of people who take the things that are going on in this world seriously and want to have engaging and meaningful dialogue that gets beyond the stupid sound bites and the absolutely asinine oversimplification of almost every event that occurs—these are the new media. Sure, not all the bugs are worked out yet, but they're coming. As Jordan Peterson has pointed out a number of times, it turns out that the American attention span is much bigger than we've been giving it credit for. I don't know about you, but I take some serious comfort in the idea. ★

The Trotskys and the Stalins

I want to start out today by telling y'all that the road to Moscow is paved with good intentions. Now let me back up and give you a little context. Have you ever heard the old chestnut "It sounds like a good idea on paper" applied to both socialism and its perfidious wet dream cousin communism? Other than "well, they've just never really been tried properly," it's about the most common thing you hear people say. So first of all, no it ain't a good idea—not even on paper. We spent over a hundred years and a hundred million lives proving that. From bread lines in Russia to zoo lines in Venezuela, from mass starvation in the Ukraine to the world's most messed up retail outlet for glasses in Cambodia, this batshit crazy belief system has absolutely nothing going for it—not even the thing that most people who buy into it *think* it does, which is compassion.

That's right, folks. The idiot kings of our industrial intelligentsia see one thing and one thing only when they try to look at socialism through a rose-colored lens: empathy. Now don't get me wrong: when it's real, the compassion one feels when one examines the cruelty and disparity purveyed by man upon man is our noblest characteristic as a species. Well, that and wet T-shirt contests, but I'm getting distracted. Ain't nothin' more powerful in the world than genuine love for your fellow man. And ain't nothin' more dangerous in the world than when you only pretend to.

But let's be fair to our largely eradicated socialist brothers and sisters of yore. Even giving them the benefit of the doubt and assuming that a large number of those people who were involved in, say, the Russian Revolution—which led to the rise of the Soviet Union and socialist communism spreading throughout the world—were good-hearted people who only wanted to help their fellow man . . . well, sadly, those folks weren't the ones who ended up running the joint. Wanting the world to be a fairer place may be a nice way to be as a person, but if you're stupid about it, there's always gonna be some lunatic with a hair across his ass ready to take advantage of your generosity and seize power.

Folks, I need you to understand the point I'm trying to make here. If someone like Bernie Sanders becomes president, I don't think he's going to intentionally start a famine in Puerto Rico. I don't think he's going to have people who oppose him dragged into an alley somewhere and shot in the back of the head. For as misguided as he is, I think the Bernster leans more toward that model of compassion than anything else—although how genuine he is about it is anyone's guess. No, the thing I worry about with Bernie—not to mention Alexandria Ocasio-Cortez here in a few years when she graduates high school—is that he's going to pave the way for someone else to come along and take advantage. Read your history, folks. People like Leon Trotsky—who probably had some genuine compassion for the workers of the world he was trying to unite—set up the kind of system where they thought they could help. Trotsky got an ice axe to the head for his trouble, and those workers got a boot to the neck that took half a century to topple. It's the Trotskys of the world who open the door for the Stalins in nine cases out of ten. In other words, I'm less worried about feeling the Bern than I am feeling the AfterBern.

This is the strongest, most self-driven, and greatest country in the history of the world. It can only remain that way if we don't give things like socialism and communism a toehold in the door. Don't vote for Bernie next year, folks. His compassion may be real, or it may be fake. In the end, it don't matter much because it won't be him instituting the complete overhaul of our political system. It'll be the guy standing behind him with an ice axe. ★

Hillary
the Hero

Folks, I was watching CNN the other day, and I suddenly realized that there is an American hero of conservative politics who goes largely and unfairly unsung in our daily lives. I'm talking, of course, about Hillary Clinton. There she was with Bill and some ass-kissing comedian—(aside) sweet gig, brother—and they were laughing and carrying on and doing all manner of funny-in-air-quotes stuff for the viewing pleasure of about half the American public. At one point, at this comedian's behest, Hillary even took a whack at reading part of the Mueller Report as if it was an audiobook. (Deadpan) Hilarious stuff.

Now remember back when I said Hillary is a hero of conservatism? Yeah, I felt a few of your souls out there trying to exit your bodies and go meet Jesus, but slow your roll. Yes, Hillary Clinton is more apt to suck the blood out of a vampire than the other way around, and yes, if she was president now, she'd have probably finished the job on Benghazi with a carpet and some bangy stuff, but hear me out. This thousand-year-old boogeywoman still inexplicably married to "Boogie Nights" over there gave us conservatives something special in the 2016 election, and I say we should thank her.

By the way, I don't mean for the presidency of Donald Trump . . . although thanks for that, too, Hillary. The Donald has done pretty squarely by the American people so far, at least as far as I can tell, but we all know he didn't stand a snowflake's chance at a public reading of *Huckleberry Finn* if he hadn't been going up against the Fifth Horse of the Apocalypse. But that's not what I'm talking about. (Smiles) Folks, every once in a while, I find it healthy to relive the night that Hillary lost the presidency because every time I do I experience a little bit of what the Germans call *Schadenfreude*—which is the amusement one feels at someone else's pain. Now I don't mean the American public out there who voted for Clinton in the election. We might disagree on our politics, but I love y'all too much to begrudge you voting a different way than I do. But the *press*! The mainstream media's reaction to Donald Trump winning that night . . . the crying and the wailing and the basic unspoken admonition to throw yourself out a window because the orange guy was in and the end was nigh . . . (fingers to face, chef kiss) . . . now datsa spicy meat-a-ball! I could watch that compilation on YouTube all day . . . hell, sometimes I do.

Now you might be thinking, "Chad, why are you going on about Hillary and the press and 2016? That's all done, right? Why can't you move on?"

I'll tell you why, brothers and sisters—because somewhere behind the cataracts, I saw in Hillary's eyes a glimmer of something that might be called hope. I know she's claimed that she isn't going to run for president again, but she also claimed she dodged sniper fire in Bosnia.

And I can tell you, folks, there is nothing I would love more than to see Hillary Clinton run again. Please, please, please, Hillary—be my conservative hero again, and deliver the American public yet another Night of the Long Faces in that way that only you can properly do. Yes, you'll have to wade through the current circular firing squad that is the Democratic primaries, and yes, you and Bernie will almost certainly end up on the dais squaring off. It'll be like Luke and Darth Vader all over again, except this time instead of Skywalker versus Skywalker, it'll just be walker versus walker.

Get your massive tub of popcorn and gallon-sized jug of whatever brand of soda you like to pour booze in, folks. This next year might just be about to get a whole lot more interesting! ★

Elizabeth Warren

Let's talk about the esteemed senator from the great state of Massachusetts for a minute. You know who I mean—the cool cat former Harvard law professor who keeps her beer in the fridge and her firewater in the liquor cabinet next to the ceremonial headdress made in Taiwan and the special edition Blu-ray copy of *Dances with Wolves*, the hip-as-a-hip-replacement old lady who probably serves up crab bisque at powwows while humming "Colors of the Wind" and winking salaciously at the back of the newspaper that long ago replaced her hubby's face in public. Elizabeth Warren—or as I like to call her, Princess Runs-With-Bad-Ideas—is a favorite right now for the Democratic presidential nomination, and she's comin' more out of left field than the baseball player whose dad purchased his spot on the team. (Pause) Sorry, Lori Loughlin.

The biggest for instance of late is this "wish in one hand, let the buffalo poop in the other and see which one fills up faster" notion of hers on the subject of higher education. Senator Warren is proposing that if she becomes president, her administration will see to it that not only will college be free to anyone who wants to go but that student loan debt will be wiped out entirely. Now I understand that when you're in a political party where you have to run against socialist windbags like our good friend Bernie

Sanders, you have to get out in front of the American people and prove that you can jump the shark not once but twice. But has she even stopped for a moment to consider what this is going to cost the taxpaying electorate in whose cookie jar she and pretty much everyone else in Washington has their fingers? A year ago, *Forbes* reported that American student loan debt was somewhere in the neighborhood of one and a half *trillion* dollars! That's trillion with a "T," folks. And every penny of it comes out of your hard-earned money, whether you sent your kid to college to get a degree in the history of tap dancing or not. Not only is this a bad investment of American capital, but it sets a bad precedent as well, just like the notion of free college in the first place does. Having the government step in and bail us out of every bad decision we make only teaches us that it's okay to keep making bad decisions. And sure, college is a *good* decision for a lot of people—but those are the same people who are more likely to pay off their own debt. You know, like responsible people do.

Listen up, Senator Warren, I'm running out of ways to refer to your fake Indian heritage that won't get me in trouble, so just hear this if you're out there: the United States of America didn't get to be the greatest power and best place to live in the world by giving its citizens a mommy to run and cry to every time things get a little tough. You want to fix the high cost of college-level education in the country? Work toward making the system more—not less—competitive. There are real market solutions to most of life's problems, and the vast majority of them boil down to getting the government out of the mess, not further into it.

And finally, Mrs. Warren, let me suggest that you smoke a little peyote. At the very least, it might loosen you up a bit. And who knows? Maybe you'll have a vision quest that'll carry you right into the White House. Anyway, that's my two cents on it. ★

Standards

F olks, let's talk about standards for a minute. Now I know what you're thinking: "Chad, why are you talking about what are by far the most superior types of cars, trucks, or SUVs ever manufactured?" But no—I'm talking about *human* standards—and specifically *double* standards. Again, I know what you're thinking: "Chad, are you referring to your strict but very un-PC double-D standards?" (Winks) Not this time.

The unswept corners of our American collective consciousness seem to be increasingly dedicated to the storage of unquenchable tribal rage. No matter where you go in this fine country of ours, you can hardly swing a dead cat around without hitting someone who constantly walks around pissed off at one half of his countrymen or the other. (As a side note, don't hit people with dead cats, folks. First of all, it's unsanitary. And second of all, you're just gonna make the dude madder!)

The most unfortunate effect of all this tribal rage on us as a people is simply this: it makes us stupid. And when we're stupid, we're easily divided from one another. Take a good example: Russians versus Mexicans. You've had people howling at the moon for the past two years that the Russians interfered illegally in our election process. Ol' Vladdy-Poo and his bevvy of bots getting out there on the cyber airwaves, changing the hearts and minds of anyone not smart enough to wear a tinfoil hat every time they logged onto Facebook. And hey, there's truth to it. Turns out that meddling in elections is kind of a worldwide sport played by a lot of countries in a lot of different ways. Even America's done it from time to time.

But here's the thing: these same people, who were no doubt ready to put strychnine in their own orange juice the morning the Mueller Report came out, will turn right around and tell you that anyone who opposes illegal immigrants being allowed to vote is a racist. (Pause) Huh?

Or how about the people who are so excited to let anyone and everyone into the country that they set up sanctuary cities—which sounds like a whole town full of churchgoing folk but IS NOT— why are those people all of a sudden so upset when President Trump decides to send the current flood of illegal immigrants their way? Come on, folks! What the hell do you actually WANT?

Now I know that asking partisans and maybe liberals in particular to make sense when they talk is about as impossible as guessing how many cheerleaders can dance in a mud-wrestling ring at once. (Long, thoughtful pause) What was I talking about?

But here's the thing, folks: it ain't just liberals who are susceptible to this kind of thinking. We all are. When we start substituting thoughtful, substantive, and *consistent* approaches to the issues we face as a society with piggishness and incoherence, it's gonna blow up in all our faces, no matter what party we belong to. Think through the issues, folks. Be consistent. And then, when you've taken the time to do that, and you're ready . . . well, tell us what you want. What you really, really want.

Now I'm wondering how many Spice Girls could dance in a mud-wrestling ring. Think I'll try to work that one out on my own. In the meantime, take care of each other, get a handle on your damn feelings, and try to get more fun out of life. ★

Trump Derangement Syndrome

Trump derangement syndrome (TDS) is a mental disorder that has been around since the now forty-fifth president of the United States, Donald J. Trump, decided to run for office. It is shared by liberals, never Trumpers, RINOs, leftists, socialist democrats, journalists, and vagina hat–wearing protesters around the globe. Critics of Donald Trump are no longer functioning as critical political opponents, naysayers, or ideological adversaries but rather as irrational and unhinged lunatics who have lost any level of rational thought. Look, maybe you don't like Donald Trump—hey, sometimes I think he'd make a great silent movie too—but does that mean you've gotta scream at the sky or go cry with a therapist all the while using unending expletives in online conversations and shunning anyone who you think may have voted for the man? People are abandoning long-time family and friend relationships and suffering from a serious case of "electile" dysfunction. Gimme a break. If you listen to TDS sufferers long enough, you'll come to realize that as of 2017, you and everyone who even thinks conservatively in America must be a racist, homophobic, misogynistic, xenophobic chauvinist with white male privilege and would've elected Hitler if given the opportunity. Or maybe you just have a different opinion. But the insults continue to flow. One dude told me the other day that I'm just Tomi Lahren with a penis. Maybe. But she's got bigger balls.

Look here, you safe-space-seeking moron, a couple of years ago Donald Trump tweeted that Hurricane Harvey was coming and that everyone needed to heed the warnings of state and local officials. One dude asked why should we take the advice of a bigot and a racist? Seriously dude and dudettes, it's a tweet. Don't get so upset over 140 characters.

Look bro, if you think you can launch into a Trump tirade wherever you happen to be out in public, you'd better check the map first. You're sorta surrounded. Now remind yourself how to behave in public. Shouting eff Trump everywhere from theaters to job interviews is just bad form. I get that Trump unexpectedly came out on top of the greatest field of 16 Republican candidates ever assembled and then beat Hillary Clinton, who had the election bought and paid for, and the only explanation you have for his winning is that he must've gotten the Russians to buy some Facebook ads. And that in and of itself is deranged.

Listen, if your president says he wants to protect our nation's borders and give us greater national security (just like every president before him has said) and you call him a racist, then you have TDS. If your president announces one of the greatest tax cuts in the history of the country and you're convinced it's Armageddon, then you have TDS. If you find out that unemployment among blacks and Hispanics is at an all-time low and you can't give credit to your president, then you have TDS. If the mere sight of your president makes your blood pressure explode, then you have TDS. If during any of those points you said "Not My President," you guessed it, TDS. If you think Kim Jong Un's sister is a lovely Olympic diplomat, not only do you have TDS, but you're exacerbating your condition by eating Tide PODS. If you think Chelsea

Handler, Rachel Maddow, and Joy Behar are voices of reason, you definitely have TDS, cultural PMS, and a raging case of MSNBC. And if your vocabulary consistently falls in the range of hyperbole to violence, then your TDS may be too far advanced to bring you back. C'est la vie.

Like it or not, gang, we are all in this thing together. Nobody seems to be leaving (including Trump), so we'd be better off to find a way to get along in a civilized fashion. I personally have exactly zero use for extreme right or left wingers as well as you social-commi-marxi-fascist any which way wingers. Therefore, I don't ever listen to them. So take a deep breath. ★

Was It Stolen?— or—Ask Not What Your Countrymen Did on Election Day

All right, you know what chaps my ass? Suede, if you really must know, but that's a story for a very different time. I'm frustrated by the indomitable idiocy of a certain contingent of American citizens who happen to reside on the left side of the aisle—you know, the ones attempting to create renewable energy by plugging a power strip into itself and staring super hard at that biology book so that they can see the watermark that says, "Just kidding—gender is a spectrum"? Yeah, those types. Recently (or a long time ago, if this is the fifth or sixth edition of this book*), these dimwits won an election and man-

---

* It will not be; this book is scheduled to be burned, erased from all server platforms, and completely erased from the memories of the five or so fools who read it.

aged to wheel a very old senile dude* into the White House. And despite the fact that their chosen savior calls a LID every time he wakes up and can't remember his name (*hint:* most days), he is nonetheless the hero they wanted and perhaps even the hero that they deserve.

But is he *my* president?[†]

I don't mean to indicate that whoever rightfully rests his rump behind the Resolute desk doesn't automatically garner the respect of the title of president—he or she (or zir?) most certainly does. But what if I think that the election wasn't fair? That it was—dare I say it? Yes, I dare—STOLEN?[‡]

DUN-DUN-DUUUUUUUNNNN!

Now let me pause here to allow the left-leaning quarter-dozen people reading this to pick their jaws up off the floor and have a moment to restrain their most basic instinct, which is to begin hurling shocked and shocking epithets in my direction—"conspiracy theorist" being the lowest of low-hanging fruit on that particular tree.[§] Settle down there, chief. You missed the two most important words in that sentence, which were *what if.* You see, the hair-trigger left—which had no such self-governance during the four years that they were claiming on a daily and often hourly basis the last guy stole the election[¶]—doesn't want you to even *consider the possibility* that there might have been hanky-panky this time around. And why? Is it because they're scared? Rolling around at night in their beds, feverish with horrific dreams, do they secretly fear that if I question the election too much, their

---

* Fact check: Incorrect. Joseph Robinette Biden, Jr., is many wonderful things, but a "dude" is not one of them.

† Irrelevant. We are the Borg, and Biden is OUR president. Resistance is futile.

‡ This is violent hate speech; the person typing this footnote literally had to finish typing by nose because the author's words caused his fingers to rot and fall off.

§ Heteronormative white nationalist cisgendered racist sexist bigoted homophobic transphobe with neck ever so red, to be precise.

¶ He absolutely did. Elections are always fraudulent when the winner is not woke.

guy is magically not going to be president tomorrow, and Cheeto Hitler* will once again emerge at the top of an escalator (at which point their only hope would be that it would catch that too-long tie right as he reached the bottom and suck him into the Underworld)?

Honestly, I don't think so. I think they know that's not going to happen. Just as those of us who were disappointed by the election results have had to resign ourselves to reality, I think the members of the woke left have also come to grips with the idea that the man they love to hate so much just isn't coming back. At least not for a few years—we'll see.

No, I think that socialist siren song of "Shut Your Piehole" stems from what I like to call the shit-for-lizard-brains. You see, it generally never occurs to a leftist that anyone could disagree with them and ever be right†—there's a short circuit in their thought process where that conceit ought to lie. And so, for you to even pose the question—could there have been enough voter fraud that this election wasn't legitimate?—tears at the very fabric of their mental universe and frightens them to no end. And as we all know, fear and loathing are often two sides of the same goofball coin. It's kind of like when you walk into a spider web: very little to no *actual* damage is done to you, but you freak the hell out and perform a mix of martial arts mastery that would make Mr. Miyagi‡ cry with pride just to get away from it.

Same thing for the lefties when you broach the subject of election fraud. They will say, with a straight face, that *no* election fraud happened despite the fact that there's never been a national election that had none. They will call you crazy, delusional, racist—whatever it takes, not to make the question go away, but to make

---

* This is simultaneously hate speech because Hitler is mentioned and RightThink because it slams "bad orange man."

† It's like he knows us.

‡ Somehow, some way, this is racist.

you, the person who asked it, go away. Because ultimately, that's what they really want. They want you to go away. Not entirely—they still want you to be close enough that they have someone to make fun of—but if you could just exist in your own little filthy corner of ignorance, that'd be grand, thank you very much.

Now I'm just a dude who wears a cowboy hat and contemplates things*—I don't know much. But that strikes me as a little bit of a double standard, and it seems pretty unfair. After all, I had to listen to your bullshit about Russian collusion for four years—hell, before the last administration, I'd never even *heard* the word *collusion*† before! I heard things coming out of lefty media types' mouths so wild even a QAnon member couldn't take them seriously. And you, my liberal friends, you just sat there and lapped it up. Why? Because it perfectly fit your narrative, which is generally about as innocent of evidence as it is possible to get. I, on the other hand, not only can't have a full and interesting discussion about the *possibility* that this election was stolen—I can't even bring it up—unless I want to feel that holier-than-thou hammer coming down on my head!

Y'all need Jesus,‡ I'm just saying. ★

---

* Read: racist.
† Also™.
‡ Only if he is the gardener. Oh crap . . . does this make me a racist?

PART II

RANTS ON CULTURE

Our Demented Drama

Comedy Lost

No one can take a joke anymore, and everyone is either pissed off at the joke or pissed off that others couldn't take it. It's a no-win and humorless situation. If you are living without laughter, then there's a mental hurdle that you need to overcome. I'm not saying that you need to be sitting in a straitjacket and howling with loony laughter in a padded cell. That's really crazy. I mean the simple ability to laugh at yourself and not take everything so hard. It's a joke, people.

The death of comedy leads to the death of a nation. I am completely convinced of this. Democracy dies in a stale room filled with mouth breathers who just got done killing comedy first. If not that, then what? What in the hell happened to the concept of *funny* in this country? It used to be that nothing was off-limits—there were no limits, except those that you chose to put on yourself, when it came to comedy. I can remember a time—and it wasn't that long ago—when you didn't have to look left and right two or three times like you were about to cross a street before telling a joke just to be sure that you didn't offend anybody. Hell, I can remember a time when the phrase "it's just a joke" actually meant something.

Have you noticed that? Nothing can just be a joke anymore. We live in a world now that's got a stick shoved so far up its own ass that the only recourse it has to anyone making jokes outside the very narrow paradigm of politically correct orthodoxy is to ruin people's careers and lives in a never-ending cancel culture–fueled Stalinist purge.

Someone once said "the show must go on," though, and here's the twisted part: it does. Despite the mental sickness that has raged through our cerebral network over the past decade or so, the show does go on. People still tell jokes—or at least they think they do. In a lot of cases, what they actually do is virtue signal to a crowd, whose response is usually a kind of nervous laughter mixed with clapping for some damned reason. I mentioned Stalin a moment ago. Did you know that when Stalin was in power, the people who attended his speeches had to make sure that they clapped for the right amount of time before stopping? And you absolutely didn't want to be seen stopping before everyone immediately around you stopped because that might be a good way to end your day—and your life—in a back alley with some friendly Soviet fellow gently applying a fresh coating of lead to the back of your head.

The power of political correctness in our society leads to far more than just the death of comedy, but there's a good reason why the death of comedy might be the most insidious result of all. You see, comedy is the last bastion of free speech when all else fails in the country. That's not hyperbole. I really mean it. The reason that free speech is so very important is because speech is an analogue of thought. The more tightly you twist the screws on speech, the less opportunity there is for free thought. And why is that? Because ideas float from brain to brain across the medium of speech—it is perhaps the greatest thing (aside from Victoria's Secret) that separates us from and puts us above the animals. No one can get inside your skull—at least not yet—and check to make sure that you're thinking what they want you to think. Without the ability to share our ideas with one another through free speech, free thought slowly begins to choke to death. And this is especially true in a society that constantly seeks to replace free thought with a sweeping intellectual real estate fertilized primarily with ideological bullshit. And I do mean BULLSHIT!

Folks, we desperately need to be able to laugh at things again. Most especially ourselves. And I hate to say it, but that includes the ability to laugh at things that may seem inappropriate to you or even to me (that's a very short list of things). The great lie our society has swallowed is that comedy is only a vehicle to promote hatred in the world. I'm telling you, though, that it is a medium with a panoply of purposes and that chief among them is to actually bring us closer together through shared laughter. Is that going to step on some people's toes here and there? Yep. Thank God! But at the end of the day, your feelings aren't more important than my freedom, and vice versa.

But what do I know? I'm white, privileged, and one funny son of a bitch. Of course, I'd say all that. ★

Bad Decisions

Friends, it is a pure sad but sometimes funny fact of life that the enormous field of human history is littered with the corpses of stupid people who made bad decisions. Yes, the customary custodians of the ilk of idiocy on full display in bygone times have carried and oftentimes even *been* the torch, stumbling their way through generation after generation and keeping lit the circus fire that we all agree should so long ago have gone out in our society. The modern Homeric equivalent to producing an epic tale in the honor of these hapless gods among men—and let's face it, it's mostly men—would be merely to assemble the team from *Jackass* and have them ride a shopping cart together over the edge of a cliff while firing slingshots at each other's nuts on the way down. Yes indeed, friends and neighbors, if the walls of society ever come crashing down and mankind steps collectively into that big Reality Show in the Sky, etched in Latin across the marble tombstone of our species will be the phrase "Hold My Beer."

Bad ideas come in all shapes and sizes, and consequently, so do the ramifications of those ideas. Maybe you build your house below sea level and the first hurricane that comes along destroys it, and we all feel bad for you. Of course, then when you *rebuild* your house below sea level and the next hurricane comes along and destroys it, we feel a little different. But that's just you, and you do you, boo.

Maybe you're a little more ambitious. Maybe you try to invade Russia at the beginning of the winter season and you end up losing millions of soldiers because they all freeze and starve to death without adequate supplies. And we would *kinda* feel bad for you, except for the whole part where Napoleon tried it the century before and had the same problem. Also, you're Hitler, and we just don't feel bad for strategically stupid assholes.

Guys, if you pick up a history book and thumb through it (and I do mean an honest to God history book and not some revisionist crap), you're bound to come across the people who got in there simply by stepping on the biggest rakes they could find. George Armstrong Custer only got into the history books because his dumb ass led 600 soldiers into battle against 7,000 Indians. He brought a gun to a bow and arrow fight and got a Lakota haircut for his trouble. And this kind of thing happens over and over. It was happening then, and it's happening today. And I'm not just talking about the people leaning hard on the left side of the rusty teeter-totter that is our government and trying to turn this country into a socialist paradise à la Venezuela—although don't get me wrong, B-B-B-Bernie and the Squad apparently never met a moronic policy they didn't like. Those lunatics climb daily to the top of the Bad Idea Tree and throw themselves off just so they can try to hit every branch on the way down.

But it's profligate in our society, and we're all prone to it from time to time. Hell, I wouldn't be talkin' about it like I knew anything if I hadn't stepped on a few rakes myself over the years. This morning I cut myself shaving because I was trying to use my phone to take a picture of myself shaving. We need a lifeguard in the gene pool! The key takeaway here is motive and minimization. Because people do dumb stuff for one of two reasons—either to get noticed or because they're legitimately dumb. Sometimes both. The first one's easy: don't make a bad decision just to get noticed or to become famous or powerful or rich. Don't do it! As for minimization . . . well, that one requires you to engage your noggin a little more often. The philosopher George Santayana once said that those who cannot remember the past are condemned to repeat it. And if you think it was Winston Churchill who said that, you're proving my point—he paraphrased it later. Read your history, folks, and learn from it. It's not good enough to try to balance on the termite-infested balsa wood crutch that is history as it's taught in our modern public institutions of learning. You gotta be curious. Find out what the idiots before you did, and then go out into the world and be smarter. Or at the very least be your own unique kind of idiot, and don't repeat the mistakes of others. ★

Genius at the Convenience Store

et me ask you a question: do you ever get sick of wading through vagrants, migrants, day laborers, panhandlers, riffraff, drifters, dead folks, and the homeless when you're trying to walk into the local convenience store to buy some high blood pressure? Well, one chain store in California said it found a way to keep loiterers from hanging around outside the store: they blast classical music. It's more effective than the previously used high-pitched mosquito repellers. The store blasts symphonies and occasional operas over outdoor speakers. Runs them right off. Apparently, Beethoven drives them right back under their bridges. The melodies of Mozart don't mix well with the minds of migrants, moochers, and lot loungers. I thought another good idea was if they changed the name of their slushy drink to "ICE" and played "America the Beautiful" inside. No store has come up with an idea this good since they put wieners on hot rollers by the register.

That's just mean! Those people should be able to stand around any business they want without hindrance. Look here, sock puppet, let me ask you a question: what's your address?

Mean? I want a 99-cent burrito that gives me dysentery. I shouldn't have to catch it walking in. Play that funky music white boys, except this particular store is owned by a Pakistani, so forget what I just said! The idea really did come from the owner. He ain't from Elizabethtown. I'll hush. Good idea!

But it started me to thinking about other things that would get rid of people you don't want hanging around. To clear the club at the end of the night, just blast the wedding march. You'll have guys running to the door faster than you can say morning after pill. Too many relatives hanging around the house after grandma's funeral? Just crank up "Another One Bites the Dust." Wanna clear out a Starbucks faster than a social justice warrior protest, just play some Michelle Wolf comedy. Cause that *really* does suck. I tried playing "It's Raining Men" to break up a women's protest, and a pride parade broke out. Obviously, I haven't mastered the science.

Let me lay something crazy on you called *common sense* for a few minutes. Would you like to be wildly successful in life? Let me give you a simple idea that will help you along the way. Be a *sellout*.

You live in a country that affords you more opportunities for success than any other place on the planet. But . . .

Has anyone ever tried to make you feel guilty for being happy? Have you been made to feel like you should apologize for being successful or accomplishing something? There are tons of joy killers in the world who want to pull your success down to the level of their potential. Jealousy is a disease of an immature mind. How dare you lose weight! How dare you get in shape! How dare you make more money! Buy new clothes! Make new friends! Make a change! Pursue anything new! Explore the potential of your talent!

A friend of mine recently got called a sellout because he made money—not much, mind you—from chasing his dreams. He didn't compromise his integrity, morality, authenticity, or principles. He just found ways to expand his horizons. But the peanut gallery wanted and expected him to keep doing what he's always done to entertain them—but only if he's never compensated for it. How dare he do something the world doesn't approve of, such as make a profit. Look here, Mother Teresa, first, I'd like to know how long you've been working without accepting a paycheck. I'm sure receiving financial compensation cheapens the value of your career, so you march right into human resources every two weeks and just give it back. I bet you said no to your last offer of a raise and screamed at your manager like a PMS-ing woman on steroids for daring to offer you a bonus. I bet you turn down every sales commission that comes your way because you want to keep your craft pure.

People claim to love capitalism but then complain if anyone besides themselves capitalizes from it. You know what's unattractive . . . people who *choose* to live in poverty and people who *choose* to remain unsuccessful. People who refuse to take advantage of the opportunities afforded them by their success.

"Alas! 'tis true, I have gone here and there / And made myself a motley to the view / Gored mine own thoughts, sold cheap what is most dear." That's Shakespeare, and according to him, you're only a sellout if you sell it cheap. How 'bout that.

So the next time someone wants to make you feel like a Judas Iscariot for chasing your dreams, just let it go . . . all the way to the bank. Let 'em complain. Let 'em call you a wannabe or a ladder climber or a sellout. But listen here, one day, when you're so successful that you're using two towels to dry your hair, they'll still be wallowing in self-pity and bitchin' about why the world never gave them theirs . . . communists. You go out there and do you in this land of opportunity, and let the naysayers keep flipping the burgers of unrealized potential. ★

Vanishing History

Remember back in the old days when people used to have actual, physical pictures of the people in their lives, and they hung those pictures on a wall instead of letting them hang out like digital ghosts in the cloud somewhere? And do you remember how sometimes you'd have a really good picture of yourself, but it had that ex-boyfriend or ex-girlfriend standing next to you? What'd you do when you went to frame that bad boy? That's right, you folded the picture over so that it cut them out (or, if you were *really* sure you weren't ever hooking up with them again, you actually took scissors to the thing). These days, I'm sure you can do the same thing with a Snapchat filter . . . and if you can't, I need to get on marketing that quickly.

What you were doing—both literally and figuratively—was cutting that person out of your life; in a way, you might have even been trying to pretend that the relationship had never happened at all. A psychologist might disagree with me, but as far as I'm concerned, there's nothing wrong there. No harm done to anyone—you just wanted that picture where you didn't have to wear your fat jeans (and before you call me a sexist, ladies, dudes have fat jeans too).

No harm done on an individual basis, but let me take you back to a similar process that used to happen elsewhere in the world.

The Soviet Union—particularly when it was under the leadership of Joseph Stalin—used to make people disappear from photos as well. They would go in and literally cut a person out of a picture and then retouch it to make it look as if that person had never been there, and then that would be the official narrative that went out, via the media, to the people. In Soviet Russia, the picture takes you. Of course, the main problem with this primitive version of Photoshop was that they were pretty often making the guy himself disappear at the same time. Picked a bad day to go ice fishing, Ivan.

So what was the point? Why go to the constant trouble of rewriting history over and over again? Because Stalin and "friends" wanted the narrative to be precisely in line with everything they were doing. More important, because Stalin seems to have realized the efficacy of driving out individual thought and reason in people by the masses. I know this sounds kind of conspiratorial—just wait, it gets tin-foilier.

There's a certain paralysis that seems to come on people in droves when they are forced to think through a difficult issue about which they don't immediately have all the facts at their disposal. We see this all the time today, and it's one of the reasons that we lean in the direction of tribalism in this country. Most of us seem to be lemmings, standing atop a high mesa and trying to decide which group to follow over which cliffside. And it isn't because we're dumb (be assured, some of us are); it's because it's complicated, and we've got enough stuff already going on in our lives.

Ready for the conspiracy talk? The mainstream media in our country are the less brutal (for now) version of what Stalin was doing during the Soviet era. Now I don't think it's a classic conspiracy in the sense that everyone with a press pass is attending secret orgiastic *Eyes Wide Shut*–type events, reciting the pledge, and then hammering out how they're going to shape the narrative in the United States. (By the way, if those parties *do* exist, can someone invite me next time?) Rather, I think the people toward the tops of these media dunghills—the ones who really *do* have a clear direction in which they'd like to steer the American people—disseminate their worldview down through the mindless, self-seeking idiots who actually communicate it to the public. And what they do is excise facts from stories, like cutting a person out of a picture. They have their own personal biases, and those biases are on display constantly—it's a cliché trope at this point that most people in the mainstream media are anything but fair and balanced.

But I think something deeper is at work. It isn't just that the media have a driving need to tell you *what* to think. They're also conditioning you *how* to think. I'll talk more in another rant about the American attention span, but it's worth noting here that one of the things modern media—both social and mainstream—have accomplished is turning us into a soundbite society. We tend to think in 30-second clips, when almost everything important going on around us has nuance and depth. As a result, we don't get very far in forming our opinions, and that's precisely where the media want us to be. Because if *we're* not doing it, then *they* can. Listen up, life is hard. Sometimes it's a tragic kind of hard, and sometimes it's a you-gotta-study-for-the-algebra-test kind of hard. You owe it to yourself and to others to spend time considering not only the stories that you hear in the news but also where you land on what's happening and why.

On the other hand, as a wise man once told me, you can't roller-skate in a buffalo herd. Think I'll go turn on CNN and see what's up in the world. ★

How Old Do You Have to Be Before Stupid Goes Away?

Since we've established that we are all crazy, offended, and reasonably unaware of history and unable to properly process information, let's try this insane idea on for size. It's one of the more inauspicious trends circling the waters of public rhetoric and obnoxiously humming the theme from *Jaws* to itself. There's an idea that's been promulgated over the past few years that the voting age in this country should be lowered to sixteen. Yes, folks, the sommelier has arrived at your table with the French accent on his lips and the white cloth draped over his arm and is proceeding to pour apple juice into your wineglass.

I'm about to say something pretty controversial—I know, I know, you're mortified and shocked in advance. But here goes: kids are stupid. And I mean *really* stupid.

It's not their fault. You see, the human brain contains a chunk called the *prefrontal cortex*, which is essentially its decision-making center. Some people's prefrontal cortex is pretty tiny (a certain congresswoman from New York comes to mind pretty much immediately); others have an average-sized one. And me? Well, my prefrontal cortex is so big I had to buy a truck just to drive it around. Also, it likes booze.

The point is that it doesn't finish forming until you're in your midtwenties. And that, very seriously, is the reason why kids are dumb as hell. Even the smart ones. They're not fully grown yet. And you'd think that'd be all I have to say on the subject. That everyone would take one look at what I just said there, do a quick Wikipedia check just to make sure I didn't make it up, and then agree: letting 16-year-olds vote is a terrible idea.

But here's the thing.

Let's say you've formed a club of 10 people. And the whole point of your club is for you and the other club members to go out and convince 10 other people of the most asinine and stupid and dangerous ideas so that they'll want to join your club, and then you'll have 20 people. And then to do it again, and again, and again. Where would you start? Obviously, you'd start with the dumbest people you can find.

But if you're smart, you *also* start with people whom others are more prone to listen to. That's where the kids come in. Every parent knows that we drag our sorry asses out of bed, through the muck and mire of our daily lives, and back into bed at the end of the night to the endless tune of kids bitching about *something*. It's a pre-req on the lonely road to a master's degree in "Please Jesus Come Back So I Can Finally Get Some Peace."

And kids are passionate, man. Especially when they're getting attention for it. Do you all remember that David Hogg kid? You know, the one who got famous for going on TV and using the kind of language that—had I used it at his age—would've landed me in the back forty somewhere cutting my own switch and trying to perform last rites on myself. That kid went on every show that would have him for months, spewing angry bile and calling for harsh gun control measures to be enacted by fiat in this country. Now it wasn't his fault: he's a kid—he's stupid. He doesn't know the first thing about guns, much less about the Second Amendment to the Constitution and why it's such a vital part of our makeup as a nation. But the media fell all over themselves propping him up, citing their bastardization of the notion wisdom from the mouths of babes.

It's getting deep, folks.

And then, of course, we have the more recent example of Greta Thunberg, whose speech in front of the UN Assembly on Climate Change should've won her handler and speechwriter an Oscar for the most grating impassioned speech. Again, not her fault. Not only is she a dumb kid, but there's other mental issues afoot, and you're going to trot her out there to be the shining light of your climate change movement? That's practically child abuse—I felt sorry for her more than anything else.

When kids are 16, they're still learning the concept of adult decision making, and they're learning it almost entirely secondhand. When you teach a kid to drive, you don't immediately throw him in a long-haul truck and expect him to go out and earn that CDL first day, do you? No, you ease him into it. And let's linger on that age-appropriate metaphor for one beat longer, shall we? Bear in mind that the whole time *you're* thinking about safety and defensive driving, that asshole's head is off in the clouds trying to imagine the biggest size speakers he can fit in the thing.

Kids aren't ready to make big decisions, and if you let them vote, we're all apt to pay a price for it down the road. You see what I did there? I ended with the whole road metaphor thing. Yeah, I'm pretty professional at this.

Maybe I shouldn't be voting either. ★

Hollywood

It's not just the media and the history revisionists who have driven us to the looney bin of ignorance. There's yet another instigator of misinformation that's insidiously alive and well in America: Hollywood.

One of the reasons we are all dumbed down is because we have allowed crazy-ass Hollywood to influence our thinking for generations now. I have no idea why we continue to fund these moronic thespians and their studio executive handlers to satisfy our thirst for entertainment and then bitch about their culturally and politically irrelevant, although revered opinions. You may say that you don't pay attention to Hollywood, but c'mon, man. If I say the names Whoopi, Madonna, Cher, Oprah, Alyssa, Babs, Alec, or Joy, you already know their political stances on a first-name basis.

And not only are they in the business of using fame and fortune to inundate us with political persuasions, but they also persecute conservatives with a malicious vitriol that rivals 1940s Germany. Anyone remember Kathy Griffin and her severed Trump head?

Don't even get me started on how Hollywood treats those with Christian leanings or people of Christian faith. Oh screw it . . . I'm already started. Buckle up.

Can somebody please explain to me how it is that Hollywood got to be one of the nastiest bullies of Christianity in this country? Is there some kind of prize given out to the members of the

Academy every year for dumping on as many God-fearing believers as possible via the box office bully pulpit? Over the course of the past century, Hollywood has become one of the great moral arbiters of our time, and those hard-drinking, botoxed sophisticates have stumbled their way up the steps to the heights of their ivory towers so that they can throw shade and bricks down on a select group of us peasants below.

And it's too late to pretend like Hollywood goes after *all* religions, at least these days. In the woke PC culture we've inherited through the sins of omission of our fathers, the only safe place to stick your spear these days is in the side of a Christian—preferably a white male one at that. And so Hollywood marches on to the tune of that particular drummer, making Christians out to be the fools, the idiots, the "special needs individuals" of the ideological world. Worse, we are often portrayed as outright evil, stuck in a forgotten time in American culture that may never truly have existed to begin with, spitting our teeth and our chaw into the same bucket as we redneck our way through the next set of violent acts we commit.

Christianity has been persecuted on one level or another for 2,000 years. And don't get me wrong—if it's a choice between being boiled alive in hot oil or having my set of values and the biggest part of who I am as a human being paraded in front of movie-going audiences in a kind of kabuki theater mental ward mashup, I suppose I'll take the verbal abuse. But what I don't understand is why it has to be this way. Why only Christianity, Hollywood? You play so fair with Islam these days that you've watered it down to a boring, half-finished magic carpet, and you tend to give decent shakes to other religions as well. Why Christianity?

I'll tell you why. Because at bottom, Christianity is what we have all around us, and most of its tenets run against the grain of Hollywood's thin skin and perverted lifestyle. Christianity is the threat because it's what's *here*. It's who the majority of us are. And if there's one thing that Hollywood loves to put up on the screen, it's self-loathing. The catechism of the woke left—who are the high priests and priestesses of the Hollywood machine—is that I will hate myself through to the other side so that I can love myself for being so righteous. But just remember this, fellow Christians: they hate us because we are a danger to their way of life. They hate us because we're strong. And maybe because, underneath all the bravado and virtue signaling, they hate us because they know we're right. ★

I'm Offended . . . Again!

Okay, let's take a break and have ourselves a deep breath so that we can analyze just how offended we are by these revelations of the crazy world around us. Sarcasm alert. Yes! I said it: I'm offended.

In fact, I'm offended, and I don't know why. But the why doesn't matter these days, does it? I just have to feel like the world doesn't embrace my point of view, and I live in shock and horror that the planet hasn't taken the time and energy to research, discover, and understand my way of thinking—or feeling—on any and all subject matters and perspectives.

I feel energized by my offendedness, and I feel like it truly makes a difference in my life. When I'm offended, I can vomit my opinions all over everyone around me. I can spew vitriol at total strangers and feel completely justified in my vindictive rhetorical retribution. How dare you state your opinion on your own social media pages without first finding out if I'm okay with everything you want to say and the words that you use to say it. I can literally read the emotion in the words you typed, and it's acerbic, acidic, and mean. Do you feel good about offending me? Do you feel big and strong for holding an opinion that makes me feel unheard and not understood? I'm offended. It makes my world work. It doesn't matter what you say; I know that you're referring to me, and that's hurtful and offensive, and I can't let it pass until you all know about it.

Being offended gives me rights, and those rights require that you care about my feelings right now more than anything else going on. I'm offended by words, and therefore, I require the world around me to invent words that sound less offensive to my sensitive ears. My feelings are sufficient evidence that everyone needs to change in order to accommodate me. You live your life that's completely different from mine, but I'm going to need you to change so that your existence completely validates mine. Stroke the ego of my sensitive inner child, please, or just shut up. And because offensiveness isn't a measureable trait, I'm going to need the world around me to remain as vanilla as possible. And I'm sorry if that offends those of you who prefer the world to be chocolate.

Damn. That felt good to get off my chest. Back to Crazy Land . . . ★

Losing
Meaning

What in the world is going on with our culture? Well, which culture am I talking about? Pick one. You are probably pretty partial to your own, so pick that one. It's changing, isn't it. Probably in a way that you don't like. You're now looking back from your twenty-first-century perspective and wondering what happened. Where are the traditions that used to be so meaningful, the customs that helped you become who you are? Kids today aren't enjoying what *you* thought was once meaningful. And you're disheartened by it. The things that matter can't keep up with the pace of your Wi-Fi. Remember things like dinner around the table that included conversation among family and friends? It has been replaced with cell phones and Facebook and Pokémon Go and Minecraft. Family meals have devolved into shake and bake fast-food consumption while the television provides background noise. Why have we gotten this lazy? We've eliminated relationships, devalued conversation, eradicated critical thinking, destroyed the concept of family, ridiculed faith, and replaced our friendships with technological mind-numbing devices. Look at you . . . right now, reading my words. Isolated and alone in your own little world.

Listen folks . . . a community is only as strong as its language and its culture, and we are rapidly losing both. When you lose those things, you lose your identity. Language and culture take centuries and generations to develop . . . slowly . . . methodically, but in today's fast-paced internet world, we don't have time for that. We've gotta get out the door to soccer, baseball, scouts, the bar, the restaurant, the meeting, on to the next, on to the next. Put down the hammer, folks, and appreciate life for a minute. Hold on to the things that matter. You can't microwave those things. They have to marinate.

Shhhhh. Breathe. Pet the dog. Ahhhhhhh. That's nice. Wait! Shit. Speaking of dogs . . . People have lost their minds there, too. ★

Therapy Pets

I know several folks who require therapy pets for legitimate reasons. I've seen them in action, and it's a wonderful thing. However, there is new legislation that's being proposed that will crack down on folks that are falsely claiming that their pets are true service animals just so they can take them wherever they want. Good. 'Cause I've seen some of those animals dragging your butt all over the airport, and I don't need Cujo humping my leg in the exit row of the plane. Only thing your dog is servicing is itself.

People are trying to drag everything into public from parrots to gerbils to fish and claiming it is because they are therapy animals. We really are *that* crazy.

Let me ask you a question: how are you gonna get a fish past TSA? It's gotta be in less than 3 ounces of water. One girl a few years ago flushed her therapy hamster down the airplane toilet. Then another girl tried to get on a plane with her emotional support peacock. Who has time to keep up with a damn peacock on an airplane?

I don't want my dog traveling with me for emotional support. My dog stresses me out. I could go online and buy him a service dog vest and even get registration papers, but it won't get him to fill up the holes he's been digging in the backyard and stop dragging neighborhood kids over the fence. My dog isn't here for that level of emotional support. He's here to eat your arm off if you mess with me. And that brings me comfort.

Look here, Cesar Millan, if you take Gigi into public and all she does is shake and cower over her nervous puddle of pee, then she's the one needing emotional support. Not you. Don't abuse the system, people. Legitimate service dogs range from guide dogs for the blind to psychiatric service animals that can sense oncoming panic attacks in owners suffering from posttraumatic stress. And unless you're actively being treated by and have a signed letter from a licensed mental health professional, don't be bringing your iguana on a plane claiming that you need emotional support. If you claim to have a service animal, then you must by definition have a proveable disability. Homesickness isn't one of them. And don't forget . . . staying home can drive you crazy too. ★

Tigers
in Texas

L et me ask you a question: did you know that after India, the state of Texas now has the world's second-largest tiger population? Yeah, you heard me right. Tigers. Just when you thought all you had to worry about was pit bulls, coyotes, jackalopes, Sheila Jackson Lee, and wild hogs in Texas, there's a new kid in town . . . tigers! Texans like to own 'em. Apparently, there's 2,000 of them because they're easy to get. Cost less than a thousand dollars. There's no strict enforcement on licensing. Leave it to Texas, where everything is better, so a tabby won't do. Just when you thought folks drove big trucks to overcompensate, Texas got tigers.

Sick of your HOA jacking with you about lawn care? Get a tiger. Tired of your neighbor's chihuahua barking at 4 am? Get a tiger. I bet you they are one heck of a deterrent for Jehovah's Witnesses. Hey brother, forget that house. They can go to hell.

Look here, Jack Hanna, I'm thinking if more farmers in the border towns got themselves a bootleg secondhand tiger or two from a Siegfried and Roy estate sale, that would cut down on the flow of illegals over the Texas border immediately. We don't need no dadgum wall! You know how many tigers we can get with $15 billion?!

How do you say "Here kitty kitty" in Spanish? Now that's reality television. Pick your favorite migrant, and see if he makes it. That's seriously the hunger games for REAL!

With 2,000 tigers in Texas, it's like Mutual of Omaha up in here. Pretty soon school districts will have to change the safety signs outside to read, "Drug, Gun, and Apex Predator Free Zone."

I read an article that said the Austin zoo had three tigers and that one of them was purchased at a truck stop by a truck driver. "Hey man, I stopped at the Flyin' J and picked up a Nut Log, a 5-Hour Energy Shot, a Merle Haggard CD, a white Bengal tiger with a mere three kills on his record, and a bag of Funyuns."

Pretty soon Texans will be taking pride in their tiger ownership. They will have bumper stickers on their trucks that boast, "My Big Cat Can Eat Your Honor Student!" Keep it up, crazy Texans. It ain't so exotic when you're getting drug down Greenville Avenue by your head. ★

Questions from a Cowboy— or—The "Am I Crazy?" Quiz

H ere are some questions that keep me up at night. I left you some space between them so that you can take a pencil and write in your own answers. Enjoy!

QUESTION: If I accidentally misgender a dude as a woman and open the door for him, is it still misogyny if it turns out that dude is transgender and identifies as a woman?

QUESTION: If I'm called a cowboy, shouldn't my wife be called a bullgirl? I feel like there's a microaggression waiting to happen here.

QUESTION: Do you think aliens are disappointed when they occasionally abduct someone who's really into butt play?

QUESTION: If I say something offensive in the middle of the woods—and there's no one around to hear it and get mad—is that thing really offensive? (More on this one later in the book.)

QUESTION: Why is it that if my wife wears one of my tee shirts, it's sexy, but if I wear one of my wife's blouses . . . well, no, wait . . . that's sexy, too. Never mind.

QUESTION: What did the horse I rode in on ever do to you? ★

Food Licking

What in the Florida Everglades–meth-mouth– doublewide trailer trash–ain't got the sense God gave a goose is goin' on around here?! People are lickin' food in the grocery store and then puttin' it back on the shelf—as a prank! (Throw hands up) Sweet Lord Jesus, come and take me now! I can't live in this crazy world no more! People have always been insane, but they're taking it to new heights. What level of nasty are you at in your life when you think that something like that is even okay, let alone a good idea? Folks, listen up. There is a bond of basic human decency that binds us together in this country, a social contractual obligation to keep our saliva to ourselves, except in cases of mutually agreed upon mouth-to-mouth face suction. And in those cases, you can be all the nasty you wanna be.

But for everything else, there's that line that you just don't cross, and people have been crossin' lately. Why? What in the world happened to you crazy people? Y'all run out of bus windows to lick or somethin'? Folks, we have a generation of kids growing up now who have absolutely nothing better to do with their time than to cause other people misery just for the hell of it. And yes, people throughout all of history have pulled pranks on one another. When I was a kid, we used to call people up and ask them if they had Prince Albert in the can.

Or sometimes go cow tippin.' Or put on high heels and a party dress on Friday night, shoot arrows straight up in the sky, and then lay facedown while they whistled back down and stuck in the ground near us. We did stupid stuff. But you know what we didn't do? We didn't open up a container of Blue Bell ice cream and lick the top and then put it back in the freezer and expect to go to heaven when we died. We didn't open up a bottle of Arizona Tea, spit in it, and put the cap back on and set it on the shelf. I swear, the end is nigh, friends. The end is very, very nigh. Look here, toxic waste, when we've reached the approximate sanitary conditions of a third-world country in the space of a few short hours, thanks to some pimple-faced, Reddit-postin', Klingon-speakin', butt-pickin' freeloader who believes in a fifteen-dollar minimum wage committing all-out crimes against humanity in such a perverse way, then, brothers and sisters, we have a problem. People are gonna get sick off this type of stuff. Hell, it makes me sick, and I haven't even eaten any of those things . . . that I know of.

The way I figure it, the motivation goes something like this: we've become a culture of gregarious isolationists, and our hierarchy of attention has shifted in the past decade and a half in order to serve our new and glorious master, social media. And social media are fueled by, among other things, outrage, which we produce in much greater quantities now than we used to. Much like road rage, where you're separated from the object of your hate by noise-canceling windshields and a few tons of steel, social media allow us to live in avatar form in a world where none of the consequences of our actions have to necessarily feel real to us. Simultaneously, the anger and the laughter and the tears that we're trying to generate really boil down to one basic human emotional need: the need for attention. Just like ice cream, human beings have a surface and then all the other stuff underneath the surface. Maybe it ain't the end of the world—these kids are gonna grow out of pulling stupid stuff like this—but then again, they're just gonna have more kids and teach them to do even dumber stuff. It's a vicious cycle.

So what's the answer to all of this? Some people want everything from now on to be vacuum sealed, but that rubs me the wrong way. Why is it that every time there's a problem, people want to spend someone else's money to fix it? Some people say that the prison time some of these fools deserve is the answer, and I have some sympathy for that idea. Short of posting that weird-lookin' kid from *Deliverance* at the end of every aisle in the store, pickin' on his banjo and smilin' all creepy at you, it's a tough nut to crack. Look, maybe the solution has been starin' us in the face the whole time. It's something I've said to parents for years, and it goes out double to you parents out there whose kids are pullin' this crap: you gotta beat that ass. Raise 'em right, and then maybe they won't be inclined to do harm in the name of a few likes in the make-believe world of social media and make my tummy feel all jiggly inside.

Folks, take care of yourselves. If you buy some ice cream, try to make sure that it doesn't have a salivary slug trail blazed across the top of it. And if you're even kind of thinking about being a part of the problem rather than the solution, and filming yourself lickin' some food and puttin' it back . . . (shout) DON'T DO IT!! ★

What Other People Think

Why do you spend your time, life energy, and focus being concerned with what other people think of you? Listen, if social media have taught us anything in the twenty-first century, it's that three-quarters of the people on the planet are idiots. I mean dumber than the rock in Charlie Brown's Halloween bag. This is just something you have to come to terms with before you ever even go out in public. So relax. Feel better. Breathe. Stop worrying about what people think of you. We live in a day and age when recreational outrage is slowly becoming the national pastime. Everyone is offended by everything, and no one can take a joke. One slip of the tongue gets you hung by the neck. If you aren't guilty of something yet . . . just give it time. It's coming. The judgment police are alive and well and out on patrol. Whatcha gonna do when they come for you?.

Look at it like this: if you're out there wanting people's acceptance of you . . . their praise, their accolades, their kind words . . . and that's what makes you feel good about yourself, then their rejection of you will destroy your life. So look here, Mr. Sensitive, don't take it so hard. People are gonna complain, and people are gonna judge. That's life. They're in your business 24/6. The only problem is that you don't know which day they're taking off. But the last time I checked, nobody rolled out a throne for anyone to sit on when it comes to looking over my life.

Take my dog, for instance. He doesn't give a rat's ass what I've got to say: "You're the ugliest dog I've ever seen." He doesn't care what I say or think about him because his self-confidence is more robust than most of ours.

We are a toxically empathetic society that needs trigger warnings and cry closets. Our colleges and universities have safe spaces and anti–free speech zones. We are at a point where we are over-rewarding people for being weak.

Guess what that creates: even weaker individuals.

Just remember, folks: the people who can't control their own lives usually try to control others. So, hey, if you want to know if you're a puppet, just look around and see who's pulling your strings. I'm a real booooy!

So go on and watch veggie tales and Rudolph the red-nosed reindeer and listen to baby it's cold outside and tell McDonald's you want the boy's or the girl's happy meal and drink out of Starbucks red cup and wear your MAGA hat to Christmas gatherings because if someone is offended by that nonsense, it's just a reminder that that they haven't gotten far enough in life to face real stuff and no one around them has been willing to slap reality into them.

Parents have mollycoddled their kids with participation trophies and overprotected them from ever experiencing loss. Add to that an educational system that wipes their noses up through grade 12 until they are released into society to spill their watery weakness all over current culture.

Those parents themselves are spoiled by living in their easy, privileged, upper-middle-class lives of luxury where many of the easily offended never had real, actual problems to worry about, making the act of getting offended their equivalent of an actual hardship in life. In other words, they literally have nothing else to worry about but microaggressions and being politically correct.

So do not allow a bunch of hyperindulged man-children who mentally never grew up because they went through grade school with "No Child Left Behind" and unearned merit ribbons bother you. These are the folks that fight to maintain dependent, immature, and entitled attitudes that other people are solely responsible for their mood and feelings, well into their twenties and thirties.

So the next time someone gets offended by you . . . you should probably just consider the source. ★

Movies Are Expensive

Well, I could've put a down payment on a Maserati, but instead I chose to go to the movies. This is why I just stay home for entertainment, people! Remember when you could go to the movies for a buck? Some of you can remember going to the talkies for a nickel. Not anymore, my friends. Is there anything more expensive than going to a movie? I'm not talking about buying stock in Berkshire Hathaway, private jets, or Louis Vuitton luggage. I'm talking about *Pirates of the Caribbean*. I stepped up to the snack counter and felt like I was negotiating the sale of a kidney on the black market. Popcorn is so expensive that you feel like a banker is going to step out of his office and ask you to fill out some paperwork. POPCORN! It's corn, people. Not sliced mushrooms or red bell peppers. It's cheap. And all you do is add heat. It cooks itself! And I have to butter it manually. Get on Google and look up Brad Pitt's house . . . that's popcorn money. I just wanted to see a flick. Not become indentured to Hollywood. Really, dude, come on! Why do you need to run a credit check before I can buy a box of Goobers? My daughters say, "Oh, let's go see *Wonder Woman*"—woman, you gonna wonder where your college fund went. *Batman* or braces, your choice, kiddo. That's it: I'm broke, bankrupt, and livin' under a bridge. Thanks a lot, matinee. ★

Take Responsibility

Well, folks, it's official: we now live in a society where no one has to take responsibility for their decisions or actions. A man sets the cruise control on his RV and then steps back to the kitchen to make a sandwich and has a wreck. What does he do? He sues the RV manufacturer. A woman spills hot coffee in her lap, and the natural response is to sue the restaurant. A so-called celebrity holds up the severed head of the president and gets blasted for it, so she apologizes not for the act but for the fact that it wasn't well received. When the apology doesn't bring the desired results, she lawyers up and blames the president himself for her actions. All this idiocy would be funny if all the scenarios were untrue. You can't make this stuff up. People get pregnant and have abortions and call it healthcare. People cram their sexuality down everyone's throats and then scream bullying. Folks preach at the world about the dangers of climate change and still drive their cars and heat and cool their homes and scream bloody murder when their power goes off at the house. In today's culture, all we do is point the finger at each other and play the blame game. ★

The Super Bowl

Sunday! Sunday! Sunday! At the Hard Rock Stadium in Miami Gardens, Florida, bring the whole family to witness two Mexican grandmas slip and slide in a mud-wrestling competition you won't soon be able to get out of your head! Step right up, ladies and gentlemen! Come for the football and stay for the Metamucil-fortified octogenarian octet in the Octagon! You'll thrill, and your kids will, too, as you collectively realize that the best way to prevent wardrobe malfunctions is to basically have no wardrobe! Enjoy the crotch cam, ladies and gentlemen, and may God have mercy on your dreams!

What's going on around here? Am I crazy, or did I witness just about the best Super Bowl game ever, punctuated by a halftime show that was like the Golden Girls Gone Wild?! I mean, it went from unbelievable suspense to unbelievable suspension in about six seconds flat, and I'm sorry, but color me intrigued by the modern miracles that science hath wrought, which were on display. Shakira and Jennifer Lopez, purveying their globular wares for the hashtag enjoyment of the American viewing public, ignited for young men everywhere the gasoline-soaked road that leads to "Mrs. Robinson, are you trying to seduce me?" territory. Hell, I'm closer to their age, and my face looked like Adam Schiff's in the mirror after I saw it. My eyes were bugged out, and my hair stood up. Whether or not anything else stood up ain't your business.

Let's talk about the game itself for a moment, shall we? Kansas City ought to rename their mascot Chief Pulls Bacon Out of Fire" because that's what they've been doing the past few games, and they did it up in spades at the Superbowl. Patrick Mahomes, who's just about young enough to be J-Lo's grandkid, led the Chiefs through an insane comeback that ended with a double-digit lead. But he did something more important than that. It's hard to believe that this need be mentioned, but old Patty-Poo actually stood through the whole national anthem. Now I don't know Mahomes's politics, but . . . oh, wait, that's the idea! I don't need to know his politics—I just like him to play a damn game and do a good job of it! So thank you, Patrick Mahomes, for doing your job and for setting a better example at the game than spectators Jay-Z and Beyoncé. In the case of the former, I guess years spent rapping about gang-banging produces no scintilla of irony when you're passively protesting police violence. And, of course, as always, in the case of Beyoncé, I'm far too distracted by the burning question: what in the hell are you doing with Jay-Z? Half a billion dudes out there ready to walk off a building for you at the drop of a hat, and you pick a four—AT BEST?!

Overall, I had a great time watching the whole spectacle. But I'm glad it's over because my blood pressure needs a little time to go down. Meanwhile, you all stay safe out there. ★

Invading
the Aliens

You'd have to be living under a rock in recent days if you haven't been reading the online chatter of people saying they want to storm Area 51. They need to see the aliens. Obviously, it's a joke, and no one is going to bum rush a U.S. Air Force test facility. But if they were . . . listen up trekkies, 'cause I've got a battle plan.

First, you're going to want to load up on cases of 5-Hour Energy drinks because this operation isn't going to be quick, kids. You'll also want to make sure that you have plenty of preprepared Hot Pockets that can remain under the supervision of the mom chaperones who are manning HQ. If you have extra Nerf darts, please remember to bring all you have. Remember, Brett and Kyle, this is a real battle we are heading into. This is not a PlayStation drill. We must get to those aliens. Now, first of all, this operation is going to be tough because you basement dwellers announced to the world and this man's military when you are coming. It's on their freaking calendars now. Jeez! So here's what's gonna happen, you future butt diddlers. We are are making our initial approach at 4 am. Wait, what am I saying? You guys haven't seen 4 am since your mother squirted you out in labor and delivery. So check that. We are going in at 3 in the afternoon. Please park your crappy cars 100 yards behind HQ with all identifying markers such as "Resist,

Persist, Coexist," "I'm with Her," "Beto 2020," and "Feel the Bern" stickers directed away from the operation. This is our exfiltration point. Please remember . . . this is an important point: clean out your trunk. We have to have a place to stow and transport our newly liberated friends from planet Z. Do not, I repeat, do not name your alien. By doing so you may assume its gender and/or engage in nomenclature bias. We are bringing them into our PC culture, so let's not get off on the wrong foot. Also, troops, do not attempt to engage your alien in romantic advances. We know the human girls hate you and you are desperate for affection, but you are not Captain James T. Kirk and this is not *51 Areas of Grey*.

But back to the operation. This will be a clandestine mission. If you get caught, there will be no acknowledgment of your existence, and we can only pray that Area 51 has a basement so that you can be incarcerated in a place that feels like home. Godspeed, soldier.

Now, depending on our numbers, we plan to overtake Area 51 by force similar to how the Gungans of Naboo attacked the Trade Federation. The U.S. military will never know what hit 'em. The Air Force has given a statement saying, "[Area 51] is an open training range for the U.S. Air Force, and they discourage anyone from trying to come into the area where they train American armed forces." They said that the U.S. Air Force always stands ready to protect America and its assets. Baloney! This is a tactic, people. All smoke and mirrors. Yes, we may experience minor casualties, but this is the day of our great alien liberation. Plus, we have a secret weapon. Several of our costumed operatives who frequent Comic-Con have already been abducted by the personnel in Area 51. That's right. We have people on the inside. Be brave, soldiers. This is our Independence Day. The Air Force will not shoot us because we don't believe in consequences for actions beyond being put in time-out.

My biggest fear isn't that the military is going to shoot you with an airborne A-10 Thunderbolt but rather that you morons might just be successful in turning an alien loose only to find out that it's one of them predators that's gonna rip all our spines out by our skulls. Good luck, kids. ★

Skinny Jeans

I want to live in a world in which men are not allowed to wear skinny jeans. Yeah, I said it. I don't care about your personal freedom. Look here, frosted tips, I'm looking out for your safety. You boys in painted on denim are killing yourselves from the nuts up. I want you to do better things with your life. Like being able to breathe. Skinny jeans are cutting off the flow of blood to your brain. Both heads are suffering. Those aren't pants. They're a long-form girdle. How'd you get those britches on, baby gap? You had to lie down and wiggle, didn't you? Then you used a coat hanger to get the zipper up. How much stretchy polyester is in them jeans, son? You're working with a 75 percent poly-denim blend. Those are NOT blue jeans. Look here, panty hose, you're suffocating yourself. Why? It doesn't look good on you. Plus, you're assassinating Little Richard? Where's the logic? Your man bun is so tight it's pulled brain cells loose, hasn't it? Where do you put your keys? How many times have you twisted a testicle just trying to walk? Where are you going in those? A Florida Georgia Line show? And look here, Louis XIII, if you weigh more than 150 pounds, roll those denim leg condoms off your body and get some real pants. You look like an inverted pyramid. We live in a country with an obesity problem and a skinny jeans epidemic. Only reason I wear jeans at all is because I look funny getting out of the truck in the parking lot of the hardware store wearing pajama bottoms. If you're a dude who considers himself to be petite, then you need to stop calling yourself a dude and make an appointment with your ob/gyn, 'cause you probably have a yeast infection. Men aren't petite. We eat. I'm a dad, and I've got a bod, and I'm going to dress accordingly. If you see me sitting down in public with my shirt untucked, I can promise you my pants are unbuttoned. Men are built for comfort, not speed. Put on some real pants, and give that guy some wiggle room. Skinny jeans . . . And don't fart in those things either. You'll look like a water balloon ready to pop.

It's the skinny jean lack of blood flow that's reducing your IQ. That's the only way I can personally justify the logic that leads you to put your hair in a "Little House on the Prairie" lady bun on the back of your head. My dad was always ready to snatch a knot in my butt. Why in the world would I wanna give him an extra hair handle? ★

Men's Rompers

What the hell is Madison Avenue trying to push on us now? A men's romper. Just say that word out loud a few times 'till it loses all meaning. The words *men* and *romper* should never be used in conjunction with one another. Men don't romp. Men don't frolick. Men don't galavant. Men don't cavort. And real men definitely don't stand around in groups taking pictures of themselves wearing said rompers. What's next . . . instead of a handshake, we'll bring on the male curtsy? Let me ask you an honest question here, free ball: if you're wearing a romper, how in the world do you insert your manpon? What'd you eat for breakfast? A little yogurt with granola? What's for dinner, a fresh garden chop and a pink zinfandel? What time does "The View" come on? I just threw up in my mouth. I never knew how much the world needed one-piece casual wear for men. I can tell you this: I didn't wake up this morning and think, "I wonder if my wife owns something I can wear to be comfortable"! It's real simple, folks. Would John Wayne or Clint Eastwood wear a romper? Well, would they, punk? Then I'm not either. Jake Davis and Levi Strauss invented blue jeans in 1873, and if they were good enough for Jesus and George Washington, then they're good enough for me. Can you imagine a grown man cutting down trees in the forest to build his rough-hewn log cabin on the frontier and his pioneer wife brings him a canteen of water and says, "Now don't overheat, Jebediah"? Not to worry, Mary Esther, I'm refreshed and cool in my wilderness rompers. Nice onesie, bro. No, what goes good with that? Thigh highs and pigtails. Might as well take the man bun to the next level there, Lady Lovely Locks. No man hunts and gathers in rompers. There, I said it. Hell, you can't even take a dump in rompers without doing Pilates in the stall, and that, my friends, is reason enough to just say no. ★

Credit Card Decline

Have you ever gone to a restaurant, store, drive-thru, or bar and tried to pay for something and your debit or credit card gets declined for some reason—for no reason whatsoever that you could possibly be aware of? Have you ever noticed the look that person gives you as he hands you your card back? That look of condescension and judgment? You know that look. Like they're trying to sort out whether they should feel sorry for you or if you're guilty of something. They look at you like they're trying to decide if they need to call security. I'm sorry, sir, your card has been declined. And then they give that apologetic look to everyone in line behind you. Like you're a fugitive from justice, and the government has locked down your accounts. I'm sorry, Edward Snowden, but do you have another form of payment? And then you get that look on your face. You know the one . . . like you're trying to do hard math or figure an amortization schedule. Hmmmm. Then you immediately feel the need to explain yourself: "Oh run it again, please, there's money in the account, hahaha (nervous laugh). My credit is good." You're trying your best to look innocent. "I just used that card an hour ago. It's a brand-new card." As if you need to validate your financial health to 19-year-old Britnee with two E's who's making $8.25 an hour working the J.C. Penney's checkout line number 6 and drives a silver '03 Nissan Sentra with hail damage. "Well, sir, maybe you could call your financial institution and step to the back of the line." So you step to the back of the line and you call your crappy bank with the name that rhymes with Wells Bargo, and they send you over to the fraud department to verify your last five purchases. And here's where it really gets embarrassing: can you verify a charge of $56.47 at Chuck E. Cheese? $71.14 at Victoria's Secret? $213.56 at Spec's Wine and Spirits? $55.09 at the Fuel City gas station? So now you look like a liquored-up pedophile running all over town wearing women's underwear. Finally, they take the routine "for protection purposes only" hold off of my account, and I make it back to the front of the line, where the same Britnee with two E's 15 minutes earlier denied my consumeristic liaison with a declined card and then asks, "Do you want to save 10 percent on today's purchase by applying for an in-store credit card?" This is why people go crazy, folks! ★

The Gwyneth Paltrow Rant

I have to ask this with full sincerity: am I being punk'd? Even now, as I speak, is Ashton Kutcher standing behind my truck with his little brown vest and his hair that needs cutting because he's a damn hippie? There's just no way that some of this stuff is real.

Gwyneth Paltrow—you know, the actress—has just released a candle that, according to her, smells like her vagina. Those of you with kids listening, don't worry. The C-word is off the table in this rant. I will only be referring to Ms. Paltrow's vajayjay, hoo-ha, lady garden, girly bits, vertical smile, kitty cat, and sleeve of wizard because we like to keep things clean around here. Now I understand that you're making an effort to stay relevant as you get a little older, Gwynnie-Pooh, and I also understand that it probably stings to be the only nonsuperhero in the franchise that's kept your name on the billboards. But hang on a minute, Vulva-Reen, you just took the letters that spell *sexy* and changed and rearranged a few to spell *nasty*. Nobody out there wants to light up a candle and fill the house with the smell of tuna! Nobody!

So here's the really frustrating part of all of this—that thing sold out faster than Mitt Romney! The things were flying off the shelves, no doubt delivered to homes not by drones but by magic winged maxipads. And do you know what that means? It means they're going to make more of them! Apparently, Gwyneth Paltrow's vagina is the gift that keeps on giving. It's worth noting that the candle on the shelf next to that one hasn't sold at all—it smells like shit.

Look, the point is that the world is crazy enough already—why do we have to make it crazier by endorsing with our dollars an idea so disgusting and stupid that it sounds like something even one of those kinky sex shops would look at and pass on? What kind of Sodom-and-Gomorrah, Last-Days-of-Rome, Fonzie-Jumping-the-Shark decadence are we living in that the hard-earned shekels we keep in our pockets can be so easily removed and shipped off electronically to some supercilious starlet who apparently believes that a candle in the hand is worth two in the bush . . . not sure that came out the way I wanted it to.

That all being said, I am gonna buy one. And for the same reason that everyone else snapped them up so quickly: I gotta know. And here's the weird thing—because nothing else about what I've just been talking about is weird: I'll be more disappointed if it turns out to just be some floral scent than if I light it and it immediately makes my toes curl and my whiskers fall out. At any rate, they should make great stocking stuffers when Christmas rolls around again. ★

The Meghan Markle Rant

What in the truck rant is going on around here?! I take a few days off to go fishing, and I come back and the whole damn world is in chaos again. To be fair—it was in chaos when I left, but I digress. HARRY AND MEGHAN! OH EM GEE, you guys! Ladies and gentlemen, Prince Harry and his lovely bride have made the decision to leave Buckingham Palace, quit the royal life altogether, and get jobs.

Now it takes a special kind of nerd to be a U.S. citizen and give two craps about what's going on with the royal family in Britain after we kind of fought a war so that we didn't have to. I'm talking a deeper than *Star Trek* kind of nerd, the guy or gal who lives not in the basement of his or her parents' house—you know, like Harry and Meghan have been doing—but instead lives in the root cellar under the basement. This pasty white cracker only comes out to occasionally steal Funyuns and Code Red Mountain Dew from his basement-dwelling betters when they leave to go fail a one-day attempt at a paper route or something. That being said, for it being a pretty lame spectator sport, there sure do seem to be a lot of these people with time and brain cells to waste because it's front-page news in the mainstream media.

And here we come to the most delicious part of this whole story. According to CNN and a bevy of other similarly informed talking heads, the true source of the tension that has led to young Prince Harry finally breaking up with Mommy is—wait for it . . . you gotta have *two* wait-for-its for this one—the fact that Meghan is black! Folks, when people say you can't make this kind of stuff up, they're obviously wrong, because that's what CNN and friends have done. But the kind of drug- and Red Bull-fueled rage with which you have to attack the foundations of sane and rational thought in order to come to that conclusion are formidable and multifarious indeed. Hell, Colin Kaepernick is blacker than Meghan Markle is! And what the hell does that have to do with the fact that she and the rest of the royal family don't get along? What, you think every time one of the bluebloods around the castle wants to play Who Can Shove a Stick the Furthest Up Their Butt, she's hauling Harry off to Roscoe's Chicken and Waffles instead? And what's she going to do now? Take him to the hood? Next time that boy shows up at the moat waiting for the drawbridge, he's going to have more bling hanging around his neck than Kip in *Napoleon Dynamite*.

Folks, not everything in the damn world is about racism, okay? And even if this was, it'd be the stupidest thing you could possibly want to follow. The royal family is a slowly fading inkstain scribbled across the annals of history; we need neither to idolize them nor to demonize them—just let them trickle away. And if Harry and Meghan want to leave the arthritic lap of luxury and try to make a new life for themselves out in the real world, good for them. Get some fresh air, kids! Go see the sights. You're not going to live to be a thousand like the Queen; take advantage of the time you have.

As for the rest of you, man, get a better hobby. Go watch some *Star Trek* or something. ★

The Return of the Jussie

Remember the great saga that gripped us for weeks when apparently Hollywood TV star Jussie Smollett was viciously attacked in the streets of Chicago by MAGA hat–wearing white dudes? It was a story that just kept on giving. Not only was it completely fabricated, but it proved yet again how crazy we were for believing his baloney in the first place. We were sucked in to the unfolding drama like moths to the proverbial flame.

Much like the ambling juggernaut that is the *Star Wars* franchise, the Jussie Smollett story continued to add episode after episode to a story that should have taken 30 minutes to tell. First there was "A New Hope for Racial Polarization," then "The Empire Actor Strikes Back," and finally we had "The Return of the Jussie" for our melanin-belaboring, Subway-munching, skin-bleached superhero of the woke left that had finally found himself having a spa day in the hot water he so richly deserved. That's right, it looked like Jussie was about to head to the big house, the clink, up the river, the calaboose. And why didn't this Hollywood elite who looked to be spending time at the Club Fed never really face any consequences for lying about what happened to him?

He lied about as well as a member of Congress, and he cost the city of Chicago a TON of money and two tons of credibility by perpetuating a wild goose chase that could best have been set to the music of the *Benny Hill* theme. Six counts of disorderly conduct hung about Jussie's neck like the noose that he conveniently wore for both style and comfort in the hour or two immediately following his dashing yet debunked donnybrook with a couple of MAGA hat–wearing white dudes who were played so convincingly by two non–MAGA hat–wearing black dudes. And who said that theater is dead?

Jussie Smollett is a tiny smudge in the corner of the gargantuan and mostly yellow paper that is American news in the past year, but it's worth noting that the thing he represents is much, much bigger. You see, what the radical left has tried and mostly succeeded at doing is painting a particular type of face on everyone who disagrees with them—namely people who lean more conservative than their ideological woke religion allows. The benefits of this are twofold: one, I get to turn you into a monster for not agreeing with me, and two—and this is the most important part—I get to feel supergood about myself because at least I'm not like you. It's a narcissistic, self-feeding mindset, and nowhere in the past year has it been better on display than with our Subway-sandwich-eating brother from another mother. You see, in a world where it actually takes some effort to put yourself in a situation where you're apt to meet the vanishingly few bigoted people out there in America, it's a lot easier to just make up a story about confronting them. After all, you know the media is going to lap it up like a dog with beer in his bowl—who isn't going to believe you?

Well, in this case, what the media got in their bowls was—ironically—antifreeze. And if you keep your eye out, you'll notice that most of them don't have a whole lot to say about poor Jussie—they're just sort of hoping this one will go away. And it will. Stories always do.

Jussie did not face what should've been coming his way from lady justice because let's face it, in America today, justice isn't blind. Instead, she peeks to see if a person lives in lefty land, and those woke bastards tend to receive the get-out-of-jail-free card. Damn shame, but it's true. Just ask Roger Stone what he got for being right wing. Only leftists can get away with their lies and deceit and soon find themselves rewarded for their troubles. Constant victims nevertheless. So persecuted.

What I'd say to those of Jussie's ilk is this: dude, you're a millionaire actor with a cushy life. Do you really want to spend it pretending you're put-upon? Pretending that what's left of racial injustice in this country applies to you? If you really want to help that cause instead of hurting it, when you get tired of your self-pity, why don't you try doing things to unite us, not divide us further? Because, let me tell you, beating yourself up and pretending that whitey did it just isn't your bag, man.

To the rest of you—don't be like Jussie Smollett. Be honest, go out there and try to be uniters instead of dividers, and for the love of all that's holy, find a better sandwich place than Subway! ★

The Golden Globes Rant

oly crap, people! Ricky Gervais just lit up all the actors at the Golden Globes like the Viet Cong dropping Willem Dafoe in slow motion—rat-a-tat-tat-tat! If you haven't already watched it, grab your popcorn, kids, and sit back deep in your seat for this one because you're about to see a bunch of Hollywood liberals' faces fall a helluva lot faster than they normally do with age, gravity, and plastic surgery. Ricky Gervais got up in front of God and the world and said the part that we're usually screaming at our TVs during these self-aggrandizing, masturbatory cringe binges, and he said it loud and proud, elevating himself in my astute estimation from writer and actor to fully human.

What a speech! Ricky basically told all the Hollywood types that they should shut the hell up about politics because despite the honorary political philosophy degree that comes out of the same Cracker Jacks box as their SAG card, they don't actually know anything in nine cases out of ten. And they certainly don't know enough to educate the American people. Let's not forget that these pampered prepubescent-acting punks are being paid millions of dollars to play pretend! And good for them! I applaud any man or woman or whatever the hell Ryan Gosling is who can go out and use the forces of capitalism to better themselves and their families. They start to lose me when they come out against the capitalism that's made them rich—I'm talking to you, Mark Ruffalo!—but whatever. Folks, let's never lose sight of the fact that memorizing some lines and looking pretty on camera doesn't make you any smarter than other Americans, and it sure as hell doesn't make you a better person. As Ricky Gervais pointed out in his speech, these Hollywood actors dropping tears into their beers over oppression and mayhem in the world are the same people working for film and television companies that are actually the ones perpetrating a lot of it. It doesn't get much more hypocritical than that.

Now, I liked Ricky Gervais before all of this, but watching that video . . . I think I fell in love with the man. Brutal honesty is what these people need to hear because I guarantee you that no one else in their tightly enclosed little worlds is giving them anything but positive affirmation—that verbal equivalent of the participation trophy. And will it change any of them? Probably not. But it's good, every once in a while, to know that there are a few people who run in these circles who aren't complete morons and who are willing to shine a light on the moronitude of the rest of them.

Look, it isn't that actors aren't entitled to have their own political opinions. Helluva lot of people died to make sure that they have the right to talk trash about this country, and I believe that Rose McGowan—for example—has every right to speak her mind on the political situation between us and Iran. I kinda wish she'd do it from Tehran instead of Hollywood, but I'm betting that even she isn't dumb enough for that. So yes, actors are entitled to have an opinion. And that's the real beauty of Ricky Gervais's speech, I think. Because, in my opinion, he wasn't talking to the people in that room nearly as much as he was talking to us, the viewers. By reminding them that their opinions are worth about as much as Myspace stocks, he was really reminding us of that. And for that, I tip my hat. ★

The Peloton Bike Rant

Welcome back to another hayrack ride that'll take you on a tour of the funny farm, folks. Please keep your hands and knees away from the edges, stay seated throughout, and make sure you've safely stowed your common-sense and critical thinking skills before the ride begins.

What the hell is going on around here? Did you see the ad the other day for the Peloton stationary bike and the supercilious skullduggery of the woke in its wake? That's right, ladies and gentlemen, our moral betters on the extreme left shouted down from their ivory Twitter that a woman getting a $3,000 exercise machine from her husband as a Christmas gift was and is and ever shall be . . . PROBLEMATIC! Surely the vilest form of sexism nestles beneath the overt and painfully simple narrative in the half minute or so we spend watching a hot, fit chick ride her way through the year into still being a hot, fit chick! Surely the husband, in an effort to get that 1 percent body fat to finally come off of her, is only unchaining her from the heater in the basement long enough so that she can ride for an hour each day.

Folks, I'm barely exaggerating the outrage that followed this ad—the company's stock shot down $1.5 billion in *three days*! People were saying that the wife character looked scared in the video. Well, of course she looked scared! She's about to commit herself to a damn spin class for a year! I get scared every time I accidentally drive by a YMCA! God forbid we have a little anxiety from time to time when we face hard things. Nevertheless, people went crazy over this ad; even the actors got involved. The dude who played the husband even had to go on national television to clarify that he's the actor and not the character. Yeah, man, we all got that part. Anthony Hopkins doesn't really eat people. Probably. But the point isn't whether or not the actor is the character. The point is that there was nothing sexist about the character to begin with.

Listen up, all you neoliberal, noncontributing numbnuts out there, a dude giving his wife an exercise bike is not sexist. It's incredibly stupid because he's just raising the chances that she's gonna make him get on the damn thing at some point, but it's not sexist. If recreational outrage is the kind of thing that turns your dials up to 11, fine. There's plenty of real stuff in the world to get outraged about without going after a company that's just trying to get by in the world and put sweaty asses on expensive sweaty seats. If you really want to get your panties in a bunch, social justice warriors, you could always find something real to complain about. Or, hell, you could just actually get on a Peloton and ride one yourself for a while—I'm sure that'll bunch up your panties real nicely. And by the way, how do you know she wasn't training to compete against a dude trying to be a woman? Now *that's* sexist! I'm triggered! I'm triggered!

These people need to pull their heads out of their butts. There's real sexism in the world, but if you go crying wolf every five seconds about stuff like this, no one's gonna believe you when you're reporting the truth somewhere down the road.

(Looking out the windshield) I just realized I'm parked near a YMCA—I gotta go, folks. ★

Pronouns Rant

Holy Jumping Gender-Bending Jehoshaphat, what the hell is going on around here?! Has the whole world gone crazy, or is it just me? Folks, I saw a document being forwarded around the other day advising people in universities and out in the working world how to head up each and every email you send so that people who reply to you don't accidentally misgender you. In short, these days instead of a family crest sealing your message to some hapless individual, you need to send them the verbal equivalent of a picture of your junk—or I guess a picture of the junk you wish you had. Whatever.

Now, since when do I need someone to hold my hand so tightly when I'm writing an email? What chamberlain in the hierarchy of the Land of Woke startled out of sleep one night with the sudden realization that I and every other literate, computer-using American needed someone to make sure that we dot and cross our X and Y chromosomes, and everything in between, lest we piss off the gods of intersectionality and get our collective and collectivist asses tossed into leftist hell—which I can only imagine must look something like a Trump rally or maybe a reading circle.

Listen, you pink-hatted pinko-commie pronoun pushers, I've got half a mind to start intentionally misgendering every man, woman, and furry I communicate with, just to tap into your postfeminist rage tanks and use your frigidity to cool the Earth's atmosphere. There, I just solved global warming while simultaneously pissing off some liberals. If that doesn't make some heads explode, I don't know what will.

Folks, the thing that this PC culture of ours consistently gets wrong is that it confuses that which should be policed externally from that which should be policed internally. In other words, things like tolerance and consideration for the feelings of one's fellow human being don't mean a whole lot if they're forced out of you. It's far better for our society to have a few bad eggs who refuse to learn—you know, in the cases where there's actually something to learn—than an entire henhouse full of uniform—yet uniformly broken—eggs who all cop to the cultural conscience but are incapable of producing anything except a stink in the long run.

The truth of the matter is that I don't set out at the beginning of my every day to offend people. Sometimes offending people is necessary—and I'll admit, sometimes it's pretty fun, too. But I don't stand there in the shower wondering how I'm going to go out into the world that day and hurt people's feelings. You know why? Because I'm not a jackass, that's why. And the truth of the matter, liberals, is that most people are like that. We possess the inner workings necessary to treat people the way that we want to be treated. We even have that written down somewhere important, in case you didn't know.

If you want to continue to work on making the fabric of our society better, don't focus on the idea of forcing people to accept what you think is the proper level of normal—believe me, it'll change in five minutes anyway, and then you will be on the wrong end of the PC firing squad. Instead, why don't you focus on doing what the rest of us hardworking Americans are doing? Raise your kids right. If you teach a kid not to be an asshole (butthead), guess what? The world will have one less asshole (butthead)! Stop worrying about what someone else is putting at the top of an email and start worrying about the words that come out of your own mouth. ★

Hunting Rant

All of y'all out there who know me know that I'm a vocal proponent of the Second Amendment to our Constitution, which grants us the right to bear arms. I also believe in the right to *bare* arms, but I don't go sleeveless 'cause my shoulders look like the belly of a fish, but that's another story. Just so we're clear on this, I don't believe in the right to carry guns simply because I like to go hunting, and I disagree with the people who try to characterize the so-called good ones among us 2A supporters as only wanting to have guns with which to hunt. No sir and no ma'am—we want to have guns so if need be, we can do some killin'. If somebody makes the massive mistake of breakin' into my house in the middle of the night, the last thing he'll see before meetin' Jesus is my naked body and a muzzle flash. And believe you me, don't nobody want to go out that way. The Second Amendment is there to protect my right to protect myself and my family from people out to harm us, up to and including my duly elected government. Hunting is just a side benefit to all that.

That being said, what I really wanted to talk to y'all about today was hunting, specifically for deer. For those of you who've never experienced it, let me tell you about how I experience it, especially at my age.

There's nothin' better in the world than waking up at the butt-crack of dawn. The room is pitch black and filled with all sorts of dark objects that you can't quite make out, and the house is quiet and still. Even God hasn't woken up yet, which is good considering what you whisper-scream under your breath as soon as your shin catches the bed corner that ain't where you left it last night. If you're lucky, you make it out of the bedroom and into the kitchen without waking your wife, make yourself a thermos of black coffee that you will profoundly regret drinking later in the day, and grab your gear in anticipation of your buddy's arrival. Said buddy will, of course, have recently installed headlights on his truck that are reminiscent of those the Coast Guard uses to scare the living daylights out of drug smugglers in cigarette boats and will park in such a way as to shine them directly through your bedroom window. You excited yet, Buckshot? 'Cause the fun part's just gettin' started.

After a short drive in which your leg hairs cook against your buddy's cab heater to the dulcet soundtrack of Roger Whittaker tunes, you're gonna spend the next four hours traipsin' through the woods in what has magically turned into the coldest winter day since the last ice age. You're gonna compose epic ballads in your head dedicated to the thermal underwear you forgot to put on under your camo and orange, and by the morning's first light, you'll have a pair of snot icicles the Red Baron would be proud of. Best of all, you won't have to put on a fake smile for very long to fool your buddy into thinking you're having a great time—your face will freeze that way after the first few seconds.

You'll be carrying a magnificent deer rifle over your shoulder, of course. And you'll strongly consider shooting your buddy and just leaving a few times throughout the morning, but you'll think better of it. And will you see a deer? You better believe it! You'll step on a twig at some point during the 900-mile hike and hear a snap. And while you're tryin' to figure out whether the twig snapped or some of your frozen toes just broke off, you'll look up to see that white puff of a tail bounding off into the forest at high speed. You won't get a shot, though your buddy will claim that he almost had one. But you'll have a story, and that's what it's all really about anyway.

Any of y'all buyin' this? I didn't think so. Folks, remember the reason that you have your guns, and don't let anyone tell you they're not for defending your home and property. And if you go deer hunting, hopefully you'll have a better trip than my last one. ★

PART III

RANTS ON MARRIAGE, RELATIONSHIPS, AND FAMILY

A Crazy Mystery

The Bathroom Cold War

Marriage and relationships will drive you nuts. From time to time throughout this lighthearted tome I want to offer up a few random reminders of the mundane day-to-day existence we've come to classify as normal. Whatever the hell normal is. Here we go.

Since when is it not okay for a man to shave in his own bathroom? We may be living in the age of beards again, but I don't like to get too scruffy before putting a razor on it—that's just how I roll. My ex-wife—the sweet, angelic peach of a woman with whom I did not but should have signed a prenuptial agreement concerning arbitration in the ablution area—always came in and started complaining at me for leaving hairs in the sink. Hairs that, I would like to qualify should this book ever show up as evidence in a homicide investigation, I was already planning to wipe up once I was done! Or at least that was my common defense.

Now I don't like to point out hypocrisy when I see it . . . oh, wait, yes I do. What about the carnage left behind in the shower when she shaved her legs? Locks of Love could have collected all the shaved leg hair from the bathtub and provided two or three wigs a week. Hell, even the girl from *The Grudge* thinks our shower's a little on the hairy side. And *I* at least clean *my* hair up after I shave . . . mostly . . . sometimes . . . but that's not the point. She just lets it fall where it may, and I find it in weird and uncomfortable places I don't even want to mention.

A quick gander at your hairbrush should be enough of a reminder that you ladies tend to constantly shed from both ends. Hair is everywhere! It's enough to drive you crazy.

Oh and woe betide me if I should ever use her hairbrush on my semibald head or accidentally pick up her razor to shave my face instead of my own. It feels like you ladies dragged that thing over a gravel road. I'll be halfway to peeling my cheeks into a human fruit rollup before I realize there's anything wrong. And by then . . . it'll be too late.

Men, this is insane relational mayhem at its cold war finest.

I don't believe in existing in a cold war. Just call me Ronald Reagan. I'm in it to win it. How do we win the cold war? We escalate, of course. You always give the "enemy" something bigger to worry about. Maybe one day she'll walk in the bathroom and I'll be shaving more than just my face. That's right, sweetheart: you've got yourself a regular Pube-an Missile Crisis on your hands now. You don't want to picture it, but I'm pretty limber. I can get my leg up on the counter and everything. Hell, I'll clip my toenails while I'm at it, and Lord knows *where* all those will go!

And the next time she's in there singing "I'm Gonna Wash That Man Right Out of My Hair," dragging a dull axeblade over her legs, and completely missing the forest for the trees—so to speak—she'll hopefully come to that awful revelation that is the *real* way the bathroom cold war ends. You ready for it? It's this: I don't care if there's hair in the bathroom! I lived in Africa for years! Hell, I went to college and lived in a dorm with other men! I've seen things that would make your skin crawl and your toes curl. You can't outgross me, but I can assuredly outgross you. I'm the United States, and my wife is the Soviet Union. And her razor is Mikhail Gorbachev. And her loofah is Boris Yeltsin. And the shower curtain is the Berlin wall. Perhaps I've gone too far with the analogy.

Ladies, listen up and lighten up. Maybe this is why you call us toxic. But it's a fact: your man's got to shave his face from time to time, and he's going to make a mess. Most likely he's going to leave it behind. If you've got one who even makes the attempt to clean up after himself, maybe take that into account before torturing him on the rack. Don't let any of it drive you crazier than you already are. And just remember, at the end of the day: we are dudes. We are disgusting, and we aren't bothered by the same things you are. We can wait you out. ★

Crazy Gets Worse with Age

Here's some real-life shit that will drive you insane: getting old. Isn't for the faint of heart. It seems that the more we age, the dumber the stuff we do. Like Velcro. At what point in life does Velcro become a preferred fastener option for your clothing. If you're at a point where you go looking for new sneakers and you think Velcro instead of laces, it's a sure sign you're getting close to the grave.

I'm at a point in life (almost 50) where I believe I have entered "manopause." What the hell are night sweats, and why am I getting them? Why does my body have more estrogen than testosterone coursing through its veins? When did I start using a truck key to scratch inside my ear—in public? I didn't do this stuff when I was 23. I just want to sleep and eat, and I can't sleep because I can't breathe when I lie down in bed. Sleep is trying to kill me. Trust me: getting old SUCKS!

I don't know if you all know this about me or not, but I don't really want to die in my sleep. I don't mean that I don't want to die in bed—I'm hoping for that—just that I don't want to die in my sleep. You see, as I got older, I found out that I suffer from a condition called *sleep apnea*, which—when translated into the common parlance—means that every night my body is like Charlie Sheen crawling up the river with a knife in his teeth trying to kill my big old bald, overacting Marlon Brando of a brain before the sun comes up. Unlike with most of the normal people God put on this Earth, my body forgets to breathe multiple times during the night, so I am cursed to spend every nonwaking moment looking like a scuba diver in traction.

When they find out that you suck at sleeping, you see, they hook you up to something called a *continuous positive airway pressure (CPAP) machine.* Now if you don't know what that is, imagine hooking up a garden hose to the afterburner of a 747 jet engine and then shoving the other end of that thing up your nose. Hang on, because the first few times you use it, you're going to think you blew your own brains out. But they—and by *they* I mean the highly questionable medical professionals at the sleep center with the thousand-yard stares and the thick German accents—*they* assure you that you'll get used to it and that you'll sleep much better. And here's the damned annoying part: you do sleep much better! Overnight I went from clocking in at about the speed of a zombie caught in the tumultuous gears of the opioid crisis to sleeping so soundly that I only got morning balsa wood. I mean I've seen dead people getting less rest than I started getting.

But you still gotta deal with something strapped to your face, shoving air up in your nose and mouth all night. Sure, it's cool to pretend to be Darth Vader the first few times. And sure, there isn't anything much sexier than waking up in the morning with elastic marks all over your face and your hair looking like you used your head as an eraser all night. But it's not all it's cracked up to be. For one thing, if you toss and turn as much as I do, you're apt to end up with that hose wrapped around your neck six or seven times, and the next thing you know, you're having to answer for why you didn't even bother writing a suicide note.

Personally, I've frequently considered cutting out the hose altogether and just running a line of PVC pipe right to my face, just to preserve my own life.

It can get worse. God forbid you're sleeping with someone who farts in bed—that thing doesn't work like a gas mask! Many is the night I find myself trussed up like a Thanksgiving turkey, tears spilling involuntarily out of my burned, reddened eyes as I realize *far* too late that my beautiful, benevolent buttercup has yet again blown the big brown horn. In times like those, I reach for the comfort of the Scriptures at my bedside and do my best to use them to fan away the fumes of the devil from the intake valve of my CPAP machine. "The Lord giveth, and the Lord taketh away" I'll say while desperately hoping this is one of those "taketh away" moments. And all the while, I'll know that when it's all over, I'm still going to get the best night's sleep ever. Life's a crazy mystery, after all. ★

The Rough Girlfriend

Uh oh, folks, I think we just located ourselves another melting little snowflake, and we're about to pop a magnifying glass over that little dude to speed the process up. In Nashville, Tennessee, the other day, a 24-year-old girl was reportedly arrested for—get this—being too rough with her boyfriend during sex. Did you know that was even possible? And by the way, we're not talking she took a meat cleaver to the guy and he's short a butt cheek now or anything like that. No, she bit and scratched him too hard, and he called the police on her.

Oh, the humanity!

Folks, welcome to the glorious age of Gen Z, a place where the biggest organ in the human body is no longer the skin, but the feelings—which I guess is *thin* skin, so it's still skin. YOU GET MY POINT!

So this girl got arrested and is now facing charges for doing something that most of us dudes would have paid for at that age if it had been legal to do so. In other words, apparently I've got a few MeToo cases that need to be litigated or at least settled out of court in retrospect. And speaking of MeToo, maybe I'm looking at this all wrong. Maybe what's good for the goose is good for the gander. How about it, ladies? Should we maybe believe all victims, even this dude, who evidently has an overcooked spaghetti noodle for a backbone? And why are we even starting out by assuming their genders? Maybe she's a dude trapped in a woman's body, and he's *clearly* a woman trapped in a dude's body. This is all too complicated—makes my head hurt.

Listen up, screwball, pull that vape pen out of your man bun and shake your head to clear your thoughts. You've got two major problems here. One is that you just sent your girlfriend to jail for something that not only shouldn't constitute a crime but for which you probably ought to be putting a ring on her finger instead of a monitor on her ankle. You pretty much just screwed the only thing that's going to be around still to screw—the pooch. So that's problem one. Problem two is this: you're contributing to the miles-long list of frivolous litigation in this country that has and continues to slowly erode our freedom as American citizens. You're helping to create case law that has the potential in the future to hamper other people's ability to get their freak on. And unlike you, *they* might actually be able to handle a little sexual healing via some well-earned scratches on the back.

At any rate, I hope you've healed up and that you've got a real good relationship with your dominant hand—because that's probably about all you're gonna be hanging out with for a while.

As for the rest of you—hey, let this serve as a gentle reminder to you from your friendly neighborhood political cowboy to always have a safe word or phrase and to never make that phrase "Don't stop." Be safe out there, you kinky fools! ★

A Silent Woman

As soon as I walk through the door, I realize I'm in trouble. I don't know why; I just know that I am. Here's how that works:

You want to know how you know you are about to get murdered and end up on an episode of *Dateline*?

When your woman goes silent.

Fellas, I want to talk to you for a minute. Now it has fallen out of fashion in American discourse to say things that may be offensive, intolerant, or smack of misogyny in any way. Thankfully, I don't give much of a crap about what's fashionable so much as I do about what's true. So let's face facts: not in every situation, but in nine cases out of ten, the woman in your life is gonna make it her God-sworn duty to talk to you until one or both of your ears shrivel up and fall off your head. It ain't their fault—God made 'em that way. In fact, sometimes that's how you know you've got yourself a keeper—when she just jabbers on and on until you're ready to throw yourself off a barn onto an upright pitchfork. Yes, indeed, all you beautiful people out there: a woman's love for a man is most clearly expressed through her mouth. (I, uh . . . I should probably rephrase that.)

Anyway, that ain't what I wanted to talk to you about. In fact, it's just the opposite. Guys, if you got a lovin' woman at home and

165

she talks your ear off all the time, you want to beware of a deadly phenomenon that can sometimes happen: the silent woman.

This is the most dangerous thing in existence.

That's right, you're just walking into the house at midnight—and you left the bar early so you could be home with her—and the minute you step across the threshold you hear it: nothing.

It's just pure silence at first. Then, as you take another step, you notice that it's deathly cold in the house. Up ahead, in the living room, you see her sitting on the sofa. She's got a blanket wrapped around her and a magazine on her lap, which she's pretending to read. You know she heard you stumble in, but she doesn't look up. And that's when you begin to realize the horror movie you've just stepped into. Then she slowly looks up at you, and says . . . nothing . . . not even a freakin' grunt.

RUN!

That's right, you gotta run, man! Get on outta there before it's too late! If you're smart, you've kept your passport and some travelin' cash in the glove compartment of your truck. Don't look back, man, you're liable to be like Lot's wife and turn into a pillar of salt. It's time to move on and go start a new life, preferably under an assumed identity.

They say that hell hath no fury like a woman scorned, and they ain't wrong. The terminator has nothing on my wife. The silent woman is the most dangerous of all God's apex predators, and you can rest assured that she's plotting your murder. In fact, during that silent time, she's probably come up with at least six or seven different ways just to dispose of your body. The bottom line is this: even though you're gonna want to address the problem with her and talk about it and even listen while she expresses her feelings—anything at all just to get her to break the silence that you normally wish for with all of your heart—don't do it!

You're walking right into a trap, and you ain't got enough blood pumping to your brain to even come close to matching wits with her. You're gonna lose, partner—it's that simple.

If only there was a way to avoid this mess. ★

Valentine's Day

Okay folks, so here's what I want to know: in our modern, woke, well-adjusted, white-male-hating, wonderful world of inclusivity and withering tolerance, why in God's name is it that our ascendant societal betters—those troubadours of their truth—have not seen fit to dispose of Valentine's Day in its entirety? Why is it that every fourteenth of February I must enter with much trepidation the digital confines of my bank account, trembling like a man in a coal mine with no canary, praying to God that I will not have to sell small arms and munitions to third world countries yet again just to afford the most costly night of my year? Where are you when I need you, cancel culture?!

Folks, the diaphanous vibe of the Valentinian experience is beautiful only on the recipient end—every year, its accrual of experiences, emotions, and criminally overpriced baubles adds an element of exponential expansion to the universe of love it has created. Therefore, I, the man, am like unto Sisyphus, pushing the boulder up the side of a mountain that gets a little taller every year. That's right, ladies, whether you'll admit it or not, it's understood by all that our job is not only to break our backs and banks to woo you on that special night but also to one-up ourselves and anyone else you know each time we do it. The way I figure it, if I take good care of myself, my wife's apt to be a billionaire by the time I croak. It's almost as if it was designed that way.

And guys out there, listen up: your woman is probably going to tell you that none of what I'm saying is true. "It's all good—I'm happy with just a pizza and Netflix on the couch." Don't believe it! It may *sound* like English just came out of her mouth, but in reality, she was speaking a foreign language to you. And the translation is this: it had better be big and shiny, and I had better not have seen it coming a mile away, and you'd better have paid a lot of money for it, and you'd better take me out to a really nice dinner to celebrate having bought it for me. See, guys, for a few weeks every year about this time, a woman gets possessed by a demon, and that demon speaks vile lies in order to try to trip you up. But be strong, and heed the words I'm telling you. If you play your cards right, that demon'll exit her body in a hot minute. And sometimes there's a little love for you on the other side of the exorcism. ★

Blame
the Dog

I wanna talk to y'all about a topic that's very near and dear to my heart—and that's getting out of trouble for things. Now it's come to my attention that the general populace has tragically begun neglecting one of the truest and best forms of extricating oneself from the mess one has made.

You gotta blame the dog. Oldest trick in the book, kids. Undoubtedly, you've blamed a particularly gruesome fart on a dog before, and it's worked out to your advantage to do so. Maybe you're old enough to have even gotten away with that old lie about the dog eating your homework. Those were simpler times. But the point is that that's all amateur stuff. And it's not that there's anything wrong with blaming the dog because you slipped out a beef biscuit that's apt to change the hearts and minds of your neighbors—don't get me wrong, if it ain't broke, don't fix it. The beauty of blaming the dog is a multifaceted and multifarious thing: the dog doesn't know he's being blamed, the dog doesn't care he's being blamed, the dog can't rat you out, and ultimately, the dog rarely even gets punished.

Dogs get a free pass from most of you. Crap on the floor. We just clean it up and let them back in the house again tonight. But here's the truth, fellas: if you crack a fart that blows the sheets off the bed and your wife knows it's you, well then you, my friend, are headed for a night on the couch and cold stares the following morning. Keep a dog in the bedroom. One of those little yappy mutts that has a skull too small for a brain to fit. Five pounds of night terror at the foot of the bed. You blame that little flatulent thing. Come on, guys, this is street wisdom I'm giving you. But I digress.

Back to my point. If all you're ever blaming the dog for is petty stuff like that, you're willfully missing out on opportunities, and you need to get your life sorted out.

What's the TV doing set on the Playboy Channel? The dog must've stepped on the remote. I got drunk last night and started a fire on the living room rug? I was drinking soda. Apparently, the dog tipped the whiskey jug into my glass . . . he even hit the button that turned on the scentsy candle with his tail—I didn't know. I fell asleep and woke up watching the live version of backdraft in the living room. We are talking next-level Rin Tin Tin stuff here. Tax evasion, you say? I don't even touch my W-2s, man; that's all on my dog!

Now, obviously, there are limitations to what you can blame your dog for, and obviously, there's a certain subtlety to the art and craft of doing it. If you're not prepared to spend a little time and effort in advance to make an elaborate and somehow believable case against your dog that will stand up in court—or at least with your wife—then don't even bother. This sport ain't for sissies. On the other hand, if you've got the fortitude of an ox and the kind of time on your hands it takes to be able to pull this sort of thing off, well, then, we're off to the races, my friend.

With a little care and a little attention to detail, you can pull off the perfect dog-blaming caper. Have a plausible backstory to explain how and why your dog could have and would have committed the deeds you're accusing him of. Limit the scope and breadth of the narrative so that the fewest number of plot holes arise in the face of questioning. And most important of all, stick to your guns, my friends. Once you've committed to blaming the dog for all your failures as a human being, you gotta stay the course.

Last but not least, don't look at this as a betrayal by man of his best friend. Sure, he's your buddy, and he follows you around like Sancho Panza while you tilt at windmills. And sure he'd take a bullet for you, if it ever came to that. But don't doubt for a minute that if he ever cracked a fart and thought even for a second that he could get away with it, he wouldn't send your ass to the dog house. ★

Smelly Women

So I just read an article from *Slate* that said deodorant is a tool of the patriarchy. Well, then, girls, how 'bout you just stop wearing it, and no man will ever bother you again. No, seriously . . . the article stated that early marketing campaigns for deodorant were designed to make women feel "embarrassed by the entire concept of perspiration." And I quote: "If you long for romance, don't let your dress offend with 'armhole odor.'"

That's right, folks. Deodorant is a symbol of ongoing systemic patriarchal oppression.

Somebody needs to call the Miss America people because not only have they done away with the swimsuit competition but now they also need to get woke enough to realize that women should stink as well. Blame the patriarchy. Liberate your femininity and tell the world that girls too have a stench.

And how about you stop brushing your teeth, too. That's something only men want you to do anyway. Fight the patriarchy. Don't shave those legs or your armpits. Live like a porcupine mated with a hedgehog. Come on, Sasquatch, nobody wants you to live underneath the subjugation of men and their oppressive desire to make you pretty or odorless. Hell, now you can just be a man yourself. Grow out that gut, girls. Belch, fart, sweat, spit chew tobacco, and make obnoxious sounds at the dinner table with your hand under your armpit. In fact, don't sit at the dinner table anymore. That's where the patriarchy wants you—sitting near the kitchen to wait on his every need. Liberate thyself, oh independant swamp-ass woman! Sit in your Barcalounger behind your folding TV tray, and eat your Hungry Man Salisbury steak, creamed corn, and potatoes like the hairy, stinky, calloused, sweaty nonoppressed liberated lady beast you are.

I'm here to demand that we shut down the sexist patriarchal beauty aisle of the local box store. Be gone, beauty counter at Nieman's. Cast thyself down, oh man-oppressed sellers of eau de toilette. Set thyself free from the patriarchy. Let the saline juices of hyperhidrosis of thy apocrine armpit glands flow like the Nile before the independent tyrannical eyes of Cleopatra. There shall be no patriarchy in thine pits!

Repeat after me: if it smells like cologne, leave it alone. Put on your patchouli, and let the world know that you have progressed beyond the patriarchy. May your bedroom be a man-free zone.

Toilet paper is also patriarchal. Why are you clogging up the streams and oceans with paper waste and fast bringing about a sewage apocalypse? A full-blown angel soft Armageddon. Use your unmanicured man claws and unmoisturized gorilla palms to wipe your formerly Brazilianed backside.

May you spend your days smelling like a construction worker on the roof of a 10-story building in July. May you enter every room just to have people wonder who brought the steamed cabbage. Smelling like a plumber's butt crack is indeed gender neutral—or so I'm told. Ladies, please let your inner outhouse free.

Soap is for losers. I appeal to your inner Neanderthal to be free from the rule of men and their desire to exploit your beauty and essence with their ogling eyes and oversensitive olfactory receptors. Come on, you liberated landfill, be free from the patriarchy. Forget progress, and refinement be damned.

Here we are folks—in the twenty-fitsy century. The age of space travel and the internet. And we want to go back to being cavemen. Or cave women. I don't know anymore. Go stink among yourselves. Me and the boys are headed down to our patriarchy club to see if we can devise more ways to subjugate women. ★

Crazy Feminists

Okay, boys and girls, it is time to say enough is enough. This septic pile of garbage parading itself around today and calling itself feminism has gotten ridiculous. So-called third-wave feminists are doing everything they can to fight men being men by violently attempting to eradicate phrases like "that's just boys being boys." Do you know why boys are boys and act like boys—because they are freakin' boys. No, we aren't saying that boys will be pigs . . . boys aren't pigs . . . so don't raise them to act like pigs. See the difference?

Look, I'm not scared of any of you . . . I've got a wife, a mother, a mother-in-law, and three daughters. I'm surrounded by so much estrogen that I'm in cycle with them. So don't sit there and judge me because I'm a man and I do man things. That's a fact. We are way beyond the whole "we need to make the same as men in the workplace" arguments. These gals don't want equality—they want control. Look here, bobbed hair and bossy wives, women have equal opportunity in this country to do whatever they want to do. They are statistically more educated and have the freedom to accomplish anything they set out to achieve. However, you have got to wake up to the fact that there is a strategy in play that wants to eradicate men altogether. They want to fundamentally change manhood. They want men subjugated and under the high heel of matriarchal society.

Masculinity isn't about wearing sexy cowboy hats like mine . . . flannel shirts with jeans and boots. Masculinity is about wearing the mantle of manhood. It's about responsibility as a father, as a husband, as a son. It's a heavy role to play and absolutely important. So look here, vagina hat, there are real women out there who aren't threatened by men. They are not listening to your street-hustling gender propaganda. It's time for the defenders of true feminism to stand up against the tactics being used to fight men and the important role they play in our culture. Those ideas are disgraceful.

Most of the men I know are supporters and lovers of women. They want to please them. Take care of them. Support them. Listen to them. Learn from them. Live with them. Go to bed with them every night and wake up with them every morning. If you are offended by any of those concepts, then you're the one with the problem . . . not the guys. Get it? Got it? Good? Don't make me mansplain this again. ★

Toxic Masculinity

There's a term that's being tossed around these days called *toxic masculinity*. Call me crazy, but I don't believe that toxic masculinity exists. There's no such thing. It's a fuzzy term.

So look here, Bigfoot, continuing to throw around terms that contradict themselves such as toxic masculinity don't do anything to help your cause. The bottom line: there is a movement among us that is doing everything it can to undermine masculinity at all costs. Toxic masculinity is an oxymoron.

You know what oxymorons are: open secrets, seriously funny, military intelligence, Microsoft works, Hell's Angels, deafening silence, found missing, jumbo shrimp, Senator Feinstein, President Biden—I think you get the point.

Men can be either toxic or masculine. True masculinity can never and will never be toxic. Masculinity by its nature is not toxic. It is not mean, it is not cruel, it is not evil, it is not abusive, and it is not bad. Masculinity in its truest form is caring and strong and protective and, in many ways, even nurturing. Yes, I've seen men act like jackasses, and yes, I've acted like a jackass myself. But in order to do so, a man has to step away from masculinity. What you call toxic masculinity is nothing more than grade A choice jack-assery. Call it what it is, but don't call it masculine.

Have you ever heard someone refer to toxic femininity? Of course not. We have a very specific word for her. Third-wave feminists who are angry and bitter and resentful are not demonstrating femininity, but we still don't call them toxic. We call them what they are. But I digress. I'm talking about dudes. You've heard me say before, and I'll say it again: hurt people hurt people. Doesn't matter if they're male or female. And just because someone does something bad to you doesn't make everyone who shares that person's same gender evil or even toxic. I've heard women say, "I'm swearing off men." No, you're swearing off jackasses. Remember, ladies, not every guy is your ex-boyfriend.

Unfortunately, for many women, it seems that jackass guys are all they attract. Do real man still exist? Yes, they absolutely do. But the problem is that we live in a world and a culture that wants to make all men villains and weak, evil, incompetent humans. Being a man isn't bad. You've heard me say this a thousand times, and as long as I am reading these grossly negligent culturally biased headlines, you're going to hear me say it a thousand more times. We don't need to redefine masculinity. We need to revive it. We need to reclaim it. We have too many boys out there claiming to be men. It's time to pull the mask off and expose the disguise. Be a man. Take a risk. Be there for your family. Be there for your children. Be there for your community. Be there for your job. Masculinity is not about how hard you can beat your chest. It's about how consistently you can show up and fill a void that no one else can. No one else can be your wife's husband, and no one else can be your children's father. No one else, regardless of gender, can do the job you were created to do. Now show up and do it. Do it with vision, do with passion, do with discipline, do it with risk. Embrace failure, embrace success, and treat both of those imposters just the same. Now do it. Go be a man. ★

Fifty Shades of Grey

L et's get something straight. Ladies! Ladies! Ladies! The *Fifty Shades of Grey* series is a billion-dollar industry. That's a verifiable fact.

There's a lot of high and mighty out there who know this good and well; they've read and watched it too. I'm talking to you, lady. You've read those books so many times you can't even read your Bible without evil thoughts because it's bound in leather.

Well . . . there's nothing wrong with *Fifty Shades of Grey*. It's just a story about seduction. Uh huh. Seduction. The reason *Fifty Shades of Grey* is so-called sexy and seductive to you is because that dude was a billionaire. You gals lived vicariously through Anastasia Steele in your own little perverted princess fantasy scenario, except instead of a prince on a white horse, you got a sexual predator who beat women for pleasure. But what the hey! That dude could take women into a room, tie 'em up, smack 'em around, and y'all loved him for it. You'd probably even vote for him if he ran for office. He's quite beguiling. Look it up.

Why, may we ask, is it so "seductive"? Because he's pretty and has money.

You can get away with a lot of stuff when you're loaded. Christian Grey flew to her in his own helicopter and picked her up. Flew her back to his 10,000-square-foot penthouse apartment and showed her WHAT? His art collection? No! He showed her his special room. Look here, pervert, if Dewayne had picked her up in his 1978 dodge pick 'em up truck and driven her to his single-wide trailer and showed her his dedicated love closet and a pair of handcuffs left over from his last DUI, then it wouldn't be a sexy story of seduction but rather a police report of abduction. Poor Dewayne. He's just trying to be fifty shades lecherous on a redneck budget.

He can't get anyone to sign his nondisclosure agreement. He just squirts on some Hai Karate aftershave and runs a comb through that mullet, puts in his good set of teeth, and heads down to the neon palace to see how many Walmart mistresses he can push into the corner so that he can cut one out of the herd.

Now, at this point, some of you are saying how dare you say that or you're already mentally typing out your defense of the fictional Christian "I smacked a girl and she liked it" Grey. Tie yourself back up and chill. The safe word is *banana*, okay?

And some of you are happy to settle for Dewayne. His safe word is *Earnhardt*. You don't know where that banana's been. You don't even have to worry about appearances when you go out together because anything goes with a sleeveless Lynyrd Skynyrd T-shirt and tobacco juice. Dewayne is sketchy, and he's not Mr. Right, but you're willing to settle because he's Mr. Right Now!

Look here, MeToo, the bottom line is the double standard. You know it exists. Don't keep pushing and promoting certain filthy rhetoric, fantasies, and illusions out into the world of literature and film and then complain when men don't live up to your so-called standards. Then, to add to the problem, you vilify men who attempt to be gentlemen and curse them when they hold a door open for you. We live in this age of social media in which all forms of dignity, decorum, and self-awareness have been absolutely lost. You get online and act in a way that you'd never act in public, but yet you claim to demand respect. You can't post drunk pics at 3 am online and then talk about Jesus Only on your twitter profile, #Redeemed. Pick one.

All the MeToo movement has truly proven is that women can be very vulnerable and at particular risk in the wrong toxic environments. It wouldn't hurt you to have a few actual gentlemen on your side. That's all I'm saying. Oh, and Christian Grey and his helicopter aren't coming into your life anytime soon either, so close that book and get your mind straight. Oh, and men . . . don't be THAT guy. ★

Push Parties

orget baby showers. Apparently the in-vogue thing to do these days is to have what they call a *push party*. Instead of gifts that benefit the baby, mom and dad have a prenatal soiree to pamper mom and provide gifts just for her. And you can have as many as you want. One for every child.

I've got a cousin back in Georgia who's on push party number 11. That's the same cousin who got arrested at a cockfight for selling chicken salad sandwiches without a food license. Obviously, she traded the cock fights for a different kind of wrestling. You know what I'm talking about?

But . . . basically, a push party is a party to reward Mom for carrying a human inside her for nine months. And Dad is supposed to give Mom a gift for doing the pushing. My wife got her gift nine months earlier when I was having a push party of my own, but I digress. You know what Dad gets at the push party. Nothin'. Nada. Zilch. Zero. Goose egg. He's persona non grata. The government has vowed to deny all evidence of his existence. He's a ghost. He already got his. Dad gets a participation trophy, atta boy, and three years of sleepless nights. But look, I'm all for it. Celebrate Mom. Celebrate life. Celebrate baby. Celebrate family. Celebrate good health insurance. Be happy now 'cause in a couple weeks she's gonna push that slimy purple squid-looking child out of her uterus, and you'll need a drink of the leftover pink champagne that Aunt Linda brought to the push party.

I want a push party for dads. We go through a lot of emotional stress too. No, we don't have to push a wet watermelon through a dime-sized hole, but that doesn't mean we don't have feelings. Maybe we need a gift card to Buffalo Wild Wings so that we can show the boys at the bar the claw marks you left on our arms and face when we were in the delivery room and told you to just relax and breathe.

We do some pushing too, dadgumit. I took a dump one time in an airport bathroom stall that I hated to flush because I thought it might be a pending world record. I did a lot of pushing. I thought maybe they'd give me a prize or a trophy or a free upgrade to first class. Maybe some sky miles. Nope. The automatic flusher took my poo baby away, and I got NOTHIN'. But anyway, you didn't need to know all that. Thank God for you Moms out there who choose to carry and have those beautiful babies. There's nothing more sacred in the world, and I'm all for celebrating the sanctity of life and birth. So here's to you, Mom. You can push party right up 'til the break of dawn. Or 'til about 9 pm, when you're thoroughly worn out. ★

The Little League Mom

Nothing is more American than Little League baseball. Hear me out.

I want to talk to you folks a little bit about religion today. Yes! I'm about to take you to church. Cool it. I'm not talking about any of the ones you're thinking about. I'm talking, of course, about the wide world of sports. Yes, ladies and gentlemen, let us walk reverently into the vestibule and make the sign of the foam finger. Let us crack open a bottle of $17 holy barley water and partake in the sacrament together as we lift up our hearts as empty vessels to be filled with the righteous indignation that comes with tribalistic team play! God bless America!

What I actually want to talk to you about is the Sunday school version of American sport—Little League. And more specifically, Little League moms. Now, I know, you've got your Randy Marsh Little League dad types out there—maybe they popped open a few beers before the game, and now they're feeling their oats and maybe want to rip off a shirt and fight. Those dudes are the types you want to be sitting a fair distance away from so you don't have to breathe in the odor of intense and mostly groundless posturing. But they're Little League themselves in comparison to the murderous Viking warrior who is the pointy-haired, UGG boot–wearing, sponsored-by-pinot-noir, suburban-driving mom. Brethren and sistren, hell hath no more intimidating force betwixt the pincers of its grasp than the matriarchal monster who has teleported from dire realms unknown to "support" her little baby out there on the field of battle.

Having laid out her unnecessary blanket on the AstroTurf sideline and erected the gantry of her folding chair, this mother has come to hold court in a fashion that would make Stalin blush. She is the queen of the realm—she subsumes the role of the coach, the players, the umpires, and the spectators all in one; she lives and breathes the sport, and no commentator on Earth could hold her jockstrap. As the game unfolds, she will scream directions to the players—every one of whose inexhaustibly weird permutations of normal names she has memorized. Her ululating battle cries will rise in decibel level and pitch, and dogs for miles around will howl at the sky, thinking they're missing out on chasing one hell of an ambulance. She is animated, throwing wild gestures in the manner of a late-stage schizophrenic, for there is a championship to be won! She paradoxically and simultaneously embodies the participation trophy and the hard-earned spoils of war, and she will force-choke the shit out of you with a look of her eye if you dare to politely ask her to quiet down so that you can enjoy the game.

Somewhere on the mantle in her home, no doubt alternating between the severed heads of her previous enemies, is every sports-related accomplishment writ solid that her darling child ever had the temerity to not win sooner. She is cyclone, and she is madness, and folks . . . I'm scared of her. God forbid the young umpire makes a call that goes against her little Johnny, because she will hit that chain link fence harder than a gnashing zombie in *The Walking Dead*.

There's one at every game.

I'd love to tell you that there's a moral to this tale, or at the very least a recommendation for how to mitigate the intense irritation of having every single game you'd like to attend as a parent be spoiled by some screaming banshee, but the sad news is . . . you just have to put up with them. Just make sure—and I say this with all the respect necessary to save my hide if I meet you in person, ladies—make sure you're not one of them. ★

The Problem with Safe Spaces

S peaking of kids, do you remember playing tag when you were young? I do. You'd get a bunch of kids together and determine that one of them was "it." Then everyone else would scatter, and it was the job of the poor person who was "it" to hunt them down and tag one of them, thereby transferring the status of "it" to that person. Then that person would try to tag someone else, and so on. The only thing keeping a semblance of order to the game was that there was a place that was designated "base." A certain tree, a fence line, maybe the side of the house—whatever it was, as long as you were touching it, you couldn't be tagged.

And inevitably, you'd always have that one snot-nosed kid who basically just *lived* on base because he was too chicken to run out among all the other kids and take his chances. His schtick was to constantly be looking like he was *just about* to make a run for it, but you and everyone else knew that he wasn't. And so, eventually, the fabric of your little ad hoc society would begin to erode, anguished cries of "no fair" would begin to arise from the populace, and you'd be forced to enact a brief dictatorial reign in order to push through a series of legislative measures prohibiting said kid—and now everyone else—from remaining on base for more than 10 seconds at a time. The motion would carry, and in most cases, the kid who had enjoyed his brief stint as the turd in the punch bowl would go home, citing important business he had there.

Guess what? These days, we have nearly an entire generation of *that* kid. They now guard the parapets of some of our finest institutions of higher learning—you know, base—and live out their lives of perpetual nonstartitude wrapped safely in a womb of their own creation.

Exhibit A: *the safe space.* Imagine a classroom where violence isn't allowed. At. All.

Oh, you're saying that that's *all* classrooms? Well, then, imagine a classroom where hate speech, homophobia, misogyny, and the like aren't tolerated. That's pretty much all of them, too? Look, don't intentionally miss my point here, dammit! Imagine a friendly, warm classroom environment where you're free from having to be exposed to ideas that you don't like, free from anything that will in any way challenge your perceptions of what's right and wrong, what's sane and rational and what's complete lunacy. A place where you are so safe you can't even have your feelings hurt, so you have to do it to yourself. Now we're cooking with gas!

Sensitivity is a commodity, folks—our society would do well to think of it in those terms. Once you've used up what genuine sensitivity you have, your spirit is emptied of it. And when that happens, all you have left is a habit of pretending that it's still there—and all the while, you're slowly turning into a monster.

There's a version of safe spaces that's a good thing, by the way. There are places like QuikTrip—a gas station superstore chain that serves these delightful steak and cheese taquito rolls that I like to call heartburn in a bag—but I digress—that have safe spaces in the back of the store. If you come in and say that someone is trying to harm you, they'll hide you back there while they call the police and wait for them to arrive. Know what the difference is between that and the kind of safe spaces you see on college campuses? Someone is *actually* unsafe. Of course, if that guy selling me taquito rolls had a shotgun behind the counter, the whole store would be a safe space, wouldn't it?

These whining, screaming, insensitive fools constitute a study in irony; they're nickel-and-diming our societal treasure trove of genuine and necessary sensitivity to what may one day be its complete collapse, all the while shooting out of the other end of their student body a kind of spray-on faux version of the stuff. It's glittery and sparkles, and it attempts—poorly—to hide the otherwise glaring blemishes on the naked face of collectivism. Get your life together, people! When are you going to wake up and smell the adulthood?

That's what this really is all about, don't you know? Growing up is hard, and a plurality of the young men and women in our country have now decided to circumvent the natural order by turning things like college campuses into eternal playgrounds. But what happens when you venture out from there into the real world? You know, when you're serving me my burger and fries at the window because your master's degree in transgender lesbian economic theory didn't land you a job at . . . well, anywhere.

Listen up, pinheads, because I'm about to give you the shortest yet most important lecture you'll probably ever receive. The world's a dangerous place, both in word and in deed, period. And the only true safe space you'll ever have is the six or so inches between your ears. People are going to tag you in life, and sometimes you're going to be "it." If that offends or frightens you, I have two words for you: tough shit. ★

Bratty Kids

know that having a kid changes your life. I get it. I have a wife, three dogs, a cat, five kids, and a vasectomy. Somebody had to end the madness. The quota was filled. I love my kids more than life itself, but here's the thing: I know you want to do all you can to protect your little angels from the big bad world and make sure they never hear the word *no*, but let me remind you that kids are like farts. You only love your own. In fact, one of the best forms of birth control is other people's kids. Go to the Chuck E. Cheese. That place keeps liquor stores in business. In fact, if you want a good business plan, open a liquor store like a block away from the Chuck E. Cheese. Youll be rich! Dads will be excusing themselves from the birthday party and running down the street. You'll have shell-shocked guys stumbling in with cash in hand saying, "I've seen some stuff today, man."

I went to a restaurant the other day and felt like I'd walked to a day care in which the army was testing hypergas on children. These little zombies were screaming and chewing through the walls. But they're just babies! Look here, Doctor Spock, we once lived in a world where the sound of a leather belt rapidly escaping the seven denim loops of dad's Levis created immediate silence and cooperation. You didn't have to hit 'em with it. They just had to hear it. Like chambering a shotgun.

And people . . . total strangers . . . would nod approvingly at you from across the restaurant because they were already thinking about it.

These days people get offended that I'd bring up such an idea, but that's only because we have a generation that's grown up with either weak or absentee men, and thus we now mistake the voice of authority as the sound of abuse. Real authority is not abusive.

Listen, you don't know this, but when you leave the restaurant with your screaming kid, people applaud. We all want to like your kids. We do. I promise. We just feel that if you don't step up your game, they have a future in the electric chair.

I see these kids losing their minds and throwing tantrums in the grocery store. "Well, he has a learning disability." Lady, look here. BRAT isn't a learning disability.

We've created a freaking child fetish in America. We worship these little snot-nosed hellions as though they're made of glass and can do no wrong.

I'm gonna play. Make sure you're wearing your helmet. Put on your pads! Do you want me to come with you? Why are we making our kids so soft? I'm not saying don't protect your kids, but I'm saying they don't have to look like the Michelin Man every time they walk out the front door. Let them scrape their knees.

Isn't he cute? No! And he smells funny. Like a mixture of piss and Capri Sun.

I grew up in the woods. We had to be able to hear the dinner bell. We entertained ourselves. Hey, look at that snake. Is it poisonous? Pick it up and find out.

It's humor, people. Deep breath.

Don't let the kids be little dictators. Don't be a slave to your little pudding people. Let them be kids. Let them have fun. Let them fail, and let them experience the wonderful gift of disappointment.

But don't let them control you, and don't let them dictate the emotional temperature in every environment you take them into. ★

Tyranny of the Three-Year-Olds

The three-year-olds have spoken! Ladies and gentlemen, we have officially modernized, monetized, and mass-produced our way into the fabled sea of troubled, intersecting human events known as *first-world problems*. The crown of Styrofoam thorns that we routinely place on our own victimized head serves really only to remind us of how good we truly must have it in this country—that we can be worried about the foolish nonsense we get around to worrying about every day.

Folks, the actor slash TV host Mario Lopez got into trouble a while back for saying that he didn't think three-year-old children should be allowed by their parents to choose their own gender. Folks on the left just about peed their britches both standing up and sitting down, calling him out as a transphobe and suggesting that he should be fired from his Hollywood TV job.

Some halfwit even took the time to edit his Wikipedia page to reflect the righteous firestorm of approbation that must always be directed at those who dare to step outside the woke narrative of our time. Lopez apologized, of course, after reeling backward and getting a good long look at the gigantic pile of deontological doodoo he'd just managed to step in. He promised that he would work to "educate" himself going forward and will be more sensitive.

I guess no one ever told Mario Lopez that the way you deal with a schoolyard bully isn't to apologize for making him want to bully you. That's not how this works! Best thing you can do for that bully is to send him home with his teeth in a Ziploc bag so that he gets the message loud and clear that you're not to be trifled with. What Lopez should have done was stand up to the tyrannical tirade of idiot voices that constitutes the majority of Hollywood and tell 'em to stick their complaints where even Oscar won't reach. Instead, he caved, and the point he was making was once again lost, even though it's a very important one. And here it is:

Folks, we don't let our three-year-olds decide ANYTHING! Zilch. Nothing. Nada. Look here, Wokey Wokerson, little kids are cute, but they're dumber than a box of rocks . . . their belts don't go through all the loops. Anything you let them decide for themselves at that age is gonna be a disaster. Your three-year-old doesn't know gender from genocide and couldn't be less interested in it, no matter what you see them doing when they're playing. They're just barely touching the tip of the iceberg in terms of learning what it means to even be a human being, let alone developing a sexual identity. You're a new kind of special if you think that kids have the slightest idea about any of that. Then again, this country seems to have quite the infestation of that brand of special these days. What's next, proud prognosticators of the morally pusillanimous Progressive Party? You gonna let these toddlers sign up for subprime mortgages and create a housing bubble? Maybe see if they'll sign a petition in favor of a carbon tax? How about some doctor-assisted suicide for 'em if they get an ouchy and are feelin' blue?

Give me a dadgum break!

Listen up, Mario Lopez, if you're reading. I get it that you're worried about bein' run out of town on a rail for having any kind of thought that even slightly deviates from what the woke left wants you to think. But here's the deal—the world moves in cycles. Society starts in flames and ends in flames. And right before that second part, it generally gets to a place where things are so decadent that the worst problems we have are the ones—are you ready for it?—the ones we make up just so we can have some. It's important to stand up for what you believe in and to hold firm when the pressure is on you to take back something you said when you know it's right.

As for the rest of you, just remember this: you can't trust three-year-olds. About anything. They're kinda like a lot of politicians: right about the time you decide they're pretty sweet and cuddly, they go and take a crap on your leg. ★

I Beat
My Kids

A long time ago, one of my kids pulled out the chessboard and set up the pieces and challenged me to a game. She looked at me and said, "You're going to let me win, right?" I said, "Little girl, you're about to get taken to school." Let me tell you something, Boris Spassky, you wanna win, then you've got to beat me. That's what winning is. Overcoming your opponent. Do you want to grow up with an overinflated sense of how good you are? You're eight. You can't even spell humiliated. This ain't chutes and ladders, punk. You may be the queen of Candy Land. Don't be bringing your sense of entitlement up here into my living room, chica. I'm about to repaint the game room with the blood of your knights and bishops, kid. You better check your mindset before you come in here asking if I'm going to let you win. We don't do participation trophies in this house. If you wanna be the best, you gotta beat the best. Woooo. It's gonna be like taking a ride on Space Mountain, kid. I'll have you at checkmate in two moves, girly mouth. You best go find Bobby Fischer 'cause I'm coming at you with a Ponziani opening followed by a Torre attack. Then I'm gonna hit you with a folding chair. I don't care how cute those pigtails are. Mean, isn't it? Nope. And guess what? Our kids don't have to win all the time to feel good about themselves. Stop *letting* them go through life without learning how to be disappointed. These days she beats me in chess quite regularly, to be honest. All my kids can. Punks probably cheat. But, seriously, my kids know how to win and lose with grace and dignity. Give your kids a chance, but don't give them everything they think they deserve. ★

Clowns Are Everywhere

The world is going to hell, and they say we have a clown situation. These are things you never thought you'd hear. But yes, America, we have a scary clown situation. So who is scared of clowns? Apparently, every damn body. There are rumors of clowns luring kids into the woods with candy in South Carolina, wielding a machete in Georgia, and threatening schools in Ohio. I told y'all all along that white people are crazy. Well, I read yesterday that Saginaw, Texas, was next on the list. You think it's smart to terrorize Texas? I even saw an alleged picture of a clown walking around a school near my neighborhood. I've got a whole box of solutions for this situation. We don't clown in Texas.

Listen up, Pennywise, if you want to get near the kids, remember that in Texas we don't trick and we don't treat; we thirty-ought-six. Even Ronald McDonald better keep his shiny red nose clean. We'll press that bozo's head between two all beef patties and make sure his clown ass goes to jail to get the special sauce. So think about that before you start smearing on the Estée Lauder and walking around like a creep. Unless you're here to guess my weight, you should know I've got a great taxidermist and a trophy room. Now crawl back into your circus tent and find some water for the elephants. We don't have time for any more clowns. We're already busy trying to decide which one to send to the White House. ★

School
Is Back

Well, school has officially started back. Or, as I like to call it, Pokémon rehab. We get to give the kids back to the department of education for the next nine months while Momma and me can get back to priorities like day boozin' and sky rockets in flight . . . booooo. Most of you won't get that.

Hallelujah, Jesus is alive, and the kids are back in school. But quite honestly I'm concerned with my kids' emotional well-being. And I'll tell you why. Have you seen these teachers standing in the drop-off and pickup lanes? Don't let that sweet gal from meet-the-teacher-night fool you. Have you seen the way they act when directing traffic every morning and afternoon? They look more pissed off than a pit bull that was just served rice cakes. Arms flailing, telling you to stop and go. Floppin' around like Michael Phelps out of water. You're trying to get the kids unloaded, and they're pointing at you like you're a suspect in a lineup. Look, teach, I know you're pissed because you've been enjoying wine Wednesdays all summer, and now you've gotta go back to usin' your fancy book learning and moldin' little minds. But ease up on the road rage. I had already been driving a car for 20 years when you were in a sorority and majoring in undecided. I got this.

Parents, remember when you could just pull up to the curb, open the back door, and yell, "Run, Forrest" without the guilt? Or make 'em walk that last mile and a half? (Sarcasm) Directing me to a specific lane and telling me where to stop? I've had these kids full time nonstop for the last three months, and you think I'm gonna slow down to let 'em out? Do you know what I had to go thru at 6:30 this morning just to get them to YOU? Bye, Felicia.

But seriously, thank all you teachers for what you do. 'Cause we don't really want to. And folks, slow down in the school zones and put your cell phones away. ★

Participation Trophies

People get upset when I discuss this subject, but then again, someone is going to get upset if I say the Earth is round, so here we go again.

I just finished an article in which the writer claimed that participation trophies are actually a good thing for kids when they play sports. She was unable to cite any empirical evidence to support her claim but only relied on her feelings to build an argument promoting her case for participation trophies. There is a mindset in America today that says if you have fun, then you won. Look here, second grade, if you had fun, then you had fun. Winning is a completely different thing altogether. Our kids should play to win, and our kids should play for fun, and they should play with an expectation of sometimes losing. Winning is important and sometimes vital, but isn't everything because regardless of our catchy sayings, we all admit that we can't learn everything we need to learn in life from always winning.

Don't get me wrong . . . I want my kids to make the other team cry. I want them to walk out of the house with the expectation of winning every single day. The goal is to come in first. However, some days they'll lose.

There is value in loss. We need to spend a considerable amount of time with our kids teaching them how to do it correctly. If there is no such thing as failure, then there would be no drive to suc-ceed. That in and of itself is all the reward you need when you lose. There's no reason to give you the dust-collecting hardware to go with it. Everyone at some point loses in life. Wouldn't it be great if we knew how to do it with grace and dignity, honor and humility, so that the next time we would push ourselves farther and harder toward success.

But in this day and age we not only give our kids a trophy when they lose, but we've made trophies out of our kids themselves. We reward behavior that should be a regular part of their lives. For instance, my city has never sent me a tax refund because I stop at every red light. It's expected of me. I don't have to be rewarded for doing the correct thing. Learn to give your kids encourage-ment and praise when and where they're needed and beneficial. Unfortunately, we as parents have become so lazy that is easier just to reward them with a physical trinket, treat, or treasure rather then have an actual thoughtful conversation with them.

Participation trophies eliminate competition. They diminish the value of hard work and winning. Competition is everywhere. It's at every turn in life. Success is not guaranteed, and you will not get your dream job just because you put forth the effort of getting old enough to get it. There will be times in life when you have worked hard to achieve your goals. Times when you have done all the right things and taken all the necessary steps. You have put in the time, the energy, the hours, the loneliness, distress, and anx-iety, and yet you still may not receive what you hoped for. That's life, and it ain't fair. But I can guarantee you that more times than not the person who has done those things will ultimately wind up at a desired place in life over the person who has been handed everything simply because they participated.

It really does not matter to me if this makes you mad. You can continue to raise your children any way you desire. You don't have to keep score. You don't have to clap when your team makes a goal or gets a hit. We wouldn't want the kids on the other team to feel bad, now would we?

You can make sure that they never experience disappointment, that they never hear the word *no*, and that they are rewarded for mediocrity and their existence for as long as you have influence on their life. But I pray that you have purchased great long-term care insurance because one day when they have influence over your life, you're going to need other caregivers. Because when we are in need of someone to change our old folks' diapers and to roll us over so that we don't get bed sores, I've got a feeling that the kid who never experienced inconvenience or disappointment is not going to be there to do it. ★

Tide PODS

'all remember when the dumbest thing we did as teenagers was drink liquor from our parents' stash and then attempt to hide it by filling the bottle with water so that they wouldn't know any was missing? Nowadays, we have jokes, memes, and online challenges about kids eating Tide PODS and filming themselves. Yeah, they are literally turning on the camera and biting into a plastic ball of laundry detergent. In the psychological land of "Hey, don't push that button and now everyone wants to push it," now comes the "Hey don't eat the laundry detergent."

Look here, brain trust, STOP. Okay? Just stop.

Besides the fact that they're highly toxic—that means poisonous, which means they will kill you. This means that you only have one life to live, and somebody paid good money for you to have it, so please don't permanently end it by chewing on something that's designed to get the skid marks out of your stanky drawers and not digested. It means *death*, kids. There's no solution. No coming back. I know you're looking for ways to impress the girl in homeroom by going viral on YouTube, but maybe kill yourself the old-fashioned way, like joining the football team. This is the twenty-first century, folks. The World of Tomorrow. Fantasy Land my ass. Put down your global attention device, kids, and get a hobby besides mind-melting video games and chewing on poisonous soap globs. Death doesn't become you. Don't drink shampoo. Don't bathe in bleach. Don't consume brightly colored household products. Even if it's just a joke, lay off the soap nuggets, kids. They are not edible. Look up the word. I feel it's important to tell you this because your IQ level has led you to believe that it's okay to eat soap. That's all. Over and out. ★

Little Kids Can't Be Transgender— or—Hold My Apple Juice

L adies and gentlemen, I have an announcement to make. For many, many years now, I've felt out of sorts with my body. I've known ever since I was a little kid that something was wrong with me, that I just didn't fit within the square footage of this mortal coil quite the way I was supposed to. Life seemed cruel and unusual to me. I longed to be different, but the difference I sought was so specific that until recently I didn't even know what it was. Thankfully—and I write this with tears streaming down my face—I finally discovered the thing I was always meant to be. The caterpillar has emerged from the chrysalis to become a butterfly.

I realized that I was never meant to go through life with two arms, so I cut one off.

Yes, there were advantages to being the way that I was born. Typing this would've been way faster, for one thing, but the disadvantages—the oppression by nature itself—was just too much to bear. Now I wake up every day, pop a Xanax for my depression, read a chapter out of my copy of *Don't Jump*, go have a nice and tearful 45-minute session with my therapist, and then am ready to jump-start my day! I'm not going to let people bullying me for being one-armed keep me down: I was supposed to be this way. I only wish someone had told me when I was a little boy that this was the cause of all my youthful angst so that I could've gotten the procedure done sooner. Who knows how much heartache it would have saved me?

Full stop.

Now, if your first impulse is to say to me, "Chad, that's clearly not the same thing," then I say to you, "Shut up. Yes, it is." *Dysphoria* is defined in the dictionary as "a state of unease or general dissatisfaction with life." And by the way, I guaran-damn-tee you that if someone hasn't already done the crazy thing, somebody's going to at some point. Life is uncomfortable for a lot of people in this world, and some of them genuinely believe they've been born into the wrong body. Back before the left got hold of this and turned it into a rallying cry so that you'd have your mouth wide open when they were shoveling their opinions from behind the horse, it was understood that people with gender dysphoria have a difficult, hard-to-understand mental illness. And most of us felt and treated them with compassion. You know . . . loved them, like Jesus would.

If I cut my arm off because of body dysphoria, the left would celebrate my bravery and throw me a parade. This is dangerous enough. Because, ultimately, at the end of the day, I'm an adult with a fully formed (oversized, in fact) prefrontal cortex, and I can make that decision if I want to—no matter how stupid it might be.

What is far, far more dangerous, insidious, and just down-right evil, is the fact that sometimes the slippery-slope fallacy isn't a fallacy. And if I had a seven-year-old kid who decided that he or she (or zir) didn't want to have two arms, that same left would turn their parade into a torch- and pitchfork-wielding mob if I said I didn't want that kid to lop off a limb.

As I've stated previously in this scholarly tome, kids are stupid. We love them more than it's possible to love anyone or anything else, and we'd die with a smile on our faces taking a bullet for them, but we have to admit to ourselves that they're dumb. And that's okay; they're supposed to be. But one thing you don't do is give the dumbest person in the room the keys to his or her (or zoop?) own future all at once. If you cut your arm off, that decision is permanent. Know what else is permanent? Chemical castration, which is what puberty blockers do to these boys.

The overwhelming majority of children who claim that they are or wish to be the opposite gender grow out of it. They go on to lead their lives and are fine with the skin they're in. When we allow the capricious whims of someone whose melon has not yet even come close to ripening to dictate permanent changes we make to their physiology, we engage in cruelty. We engage in child abuse.

I just know some fine, sunny morning I'm gonna be standing out on my lawn, looking up at a giant asteroid about to hit the planet, and thinking, "Ah, shit. This was for that transgender kid thing, wasn't it?" ★

I'm Hiding from My Wife

I'm hiding out in a hotel room, and I'll tell you why: I'm hiding from my wife.

The new year has begun, and for many of us, that means a new resolution to lose weight and start getting ready for that beach body you had when you were 18. At my age, I don't exercise to look good. Nobody's looking. I exercise to survive. But admittedly now that I'm operating with 0 percent body muscle and an estrogen-infused dad belly, I decided I need to drop a few pounds. My genius wife said I should try a juice cleanse. I asked her if it involved whiskey, and she said, "No." So I said I don't want it. Next thing I know we are at the grocery store shopping in the fruits and vegetable aisle. I didn't know grocery stores had some of this stuff. We spent $125 on carrots, celery, cucumbers, apples, kale, bok choi, and a cup. Then she said we had to go to a specialty grocery store to buy the rest of the stuff we needed. Apparently, this store contains healthy ingredients that are harvested from interplanetary alien colonies. Some of these vegetables had legs on them and breathed. I didn't want to bring up the FACT that every one of the healthy shoppers in this store looked like they were one step away from a granola overdose and death. We took all this crap home and threw it in a blender along with a handful of fescue and St. Augustine grasses, whey protein, soy milk, ginger, parsley, aloe vera, and a banana and created what reminded me of south Louisiana swamp water. She said, "Drink it." I felt like I'd lost a bet. I stuck it in front of the dog's nose, and he whimpered and went to the corner. I manned up and chugged it and learned 12 hours later why they call it a smoothie. So I'm out on the cleanse thing. ★

Don't Call
Her Pretty

ack in the 90s, we used to make jokes about the absurdity of political correctness. Today people live in fear of losing their job over it. No one knows anymore what is deemed appropriate or inappropriate. Just last week a friend in Los Angeles told me that he was rebuked by his cousin at a party for innocently mentioning that a girl was pretty. His cousin told him he could say she was smart or accomplished or humorous, but you can't say she's pretty because that's sexually objectifying her. I said, "Well, Bubba, that logic ain't gonna fly in Texas . . . well, maybe in Austin or parts of Dallas." Texas women don't mind being called pretty. You know why? Because when they were growing up, their daddies told them they were pretty, and they don't get their switches flipped if some random guy mentions it. No, that rule was made up by some gal who's never been told she's pretty, so she and her cronies decided to make it socially illegal for anyone else to be described as such. How dare you? Oh, I dare, sister, I daaaare. If you get offended because someone tells you you're pretty, then you probably lick windows with the stupid kids.

The thought Nazis are on patrol, folks. Go to a public place and say loudly, "I love Jesus," and watch people cringe and run for cover. These are the same folks you'll see in church on Sunday singing songs, but say that in public and watch their butts pucker.

Instead, go yell out that you support gay marriage in public, and strangers will shake your hand and buy you lunch.

Welcome to the twenty-first century, folks. Kids can't play cowboys and indians. Men are oppressors. Women are survivors of objectification and sexism. Bald folks are follicly disadvantaged, and blind people are optically challenged. Black people are African Americans, even if they're from Canada, and white people are pigment impoverished. Making fun of yoga pants, UGG boots, or pumpkin-spiced lattes is sexist. You're not an American. You're a resident of the United States. Try singing that one, Toby Keith. And God forbid you ever refer to someone using a personal pronoun. Microaggressions like that make the polar ice caps melt faster.

Anyway, ladies, you *are* pretty. I hope that you can live with that offensive fact. As for me, I'm headed to the Target store to take a poop in the bathroom that identifies as belonging to females. Because I can. Hope it's not offensive. ★

Man Is King of His Home

Hey, folks, I just wanted to take a few minutes to set something straight with y'all. Those of you familiar with me know that I don't generally deign to align my silver tongue so that it plugs neatly into the politically correct outlet and that I'm just fine with the notion of pissin' off the easily offended among my brethren and sistren if it means I've had the opportunity to tell the truth as I see it. I love y'all too much to lie and spare your feelings.

So let's get this boat in the water and set sail already: the man is the king of the home. Easy there, y'all, I can feel ya breathin' down my neck through the camera. Yeah, I said it: the man is the king of his home. He's the big cheese, the boss. When the man is home, his house takes on the quality of a castle, a fortification against the dangers of the wide outside world, and he is the unquestionable master of all he surveys. From the bedroom to the laundry room, from the garage to the kitchen, from the refrigerator that purveys the cold beer to the television that purveys the sporting events, to the couch that is the mighty throne from which he rules—the man wields his power with an iron fist.

That's right, folks. When the man is home, the kids don't dare act up. (Getting fired up) Woe betide you children if you disturb the well-earned peace and quiet of the man when he is at home!

God help ya if you give him cause to rise from his couch of comfort, calling out in a loud voice as the tip of his belt breaks the sound barrier exiting the belt loops! Good Lord! What a bad night for you if you disturb the king when he's at home in his castle!

(Pause) But the man is also gentle and kind at times. He is magnanimous in his absolute rule and will sometimes reward the fetching of a beer or the opening of a bag of pretzels with an "Attaboy" or a "Thanks, but you're blockin' the TV." In these cases, as much as it would be appropriate for the children to fall to their knees and thank the man for not using his superior strength and intelligence to destroy them, it's usually better if they just quietly nod their heads and bow out of the room and then go do something useful and quiet.

Even the dog knows that when the man is home, the man is master. He will come when called and will lie faithfully on the couch at the man's side and will not fart in the man's direction while he is trying to watch sports.

Yes, truly, when the man is home, he is in charge!

Until the woman comes home.

Then, of course, the man—who has been working so hard to maintain the order and balance of the home while she was away—is nevertheless ready to work much harder. He will spring up from his throne before she walks in if he's lucky enough to hear her in the driveway and will begin doing the dishes and the laundry at the same time while simultaneously eating an unpeeled clove of garlic in an attempt to remove the smell of beer from his breath.

This is not out of fear, ladies! It's out of pure love that we rush to the bathroom and plunge that toilet that we left clogged earlier! It's out of simple adulation that we have half a bottle of lotion squeezed out into one hand and your bare foot in the other five minutes after you walk into the room. And it is a consequence of nothing but a man's sense of command responsibility that we may present you with the promise that we will accompany you to go shopping for clothes, even though inside we know that we would rather eat a bowl of grenades for breakfast than do so.

Just to be clear, we're the boss . . . but you can take over when you come home. I love y'all; take care of yourselves. ★

Forgiveness: The Final Word That Matters— or—Wake Up to the Woke— It's Gonna Kill Us All

ancel culture in the twenty-first century is nothing but an analogue for the kind of revolution where people get their heads chopped off in the public square—and that's merely because we haven't gotten back to that point yet. There, I said it: fight me. In the course of boiling our society's motivations and mores down to their most basic elements, we've created a world in which nuance is not only *not* considered when we go to judge someone who's stepped out of bounds, but in fact it's forbidden to do so. Make no mistake, that's by design; it's a fail-safe mechanism to protect against the most dangerous thing that can happen to woke ideology: free thought.

You see, one of the many problems with wokeism is that it absolutely does not stand up to even the slightest amount of scrutiny—it's a house of cards sitting on a washing machine over a pissed-off fault line: blow the tiniest breath of a genuine thought in its direction, and it falls apart. This is why its adherents must be so strident, so loud and angry all the time. If you don't really have a solid argument for why you believe what you believe, the only way you can continue to believe it (and get others to believe it as well) is to yell about it at the top of your lungs. It lends what you're saying a kind of faux credibility or, at the very least, drowns out anything anyone else is saying.

You have to understand that this is the way things go in order to be able to wrap your head around the cancel culture—otherwise, it makes no sense. Take this observation for example: how is it that many of the same people who rant and rave about the glories of criminal justice reform will, in the same breath, call for the absolute cancellation of an actor who doesn't spout *precisely* the right orthodoxy all the time. Think about that for a second, because this isn't just some sweeping generalization to make a point. Imagine containing within your skull the drive to both let a murderer go free and simultaneously the drive to do everything you can to destroy the life of someone who doesn't happen to agree with you. I'll reiterate: it's because the person who doesn't agree with you contains within their rhetoric the power to knock your entire ideology over on its side. And it's not hard.

You see, like most people, I used to think that the only reason cancel culture existed was because the little snowflakes who participate in it just couldn't stand to have their little feelies hurt. And I still think there's some truth to that, but unfortunately, the deeper reason is far more insidious.

So, with all of that in mind, let's consider a concept we should all be interested in: forgiveness.

It happens in the blink of an eye: there you are, participating in the ancient dance of language with one or more of your fellow human beings, when all of a sudden something comes out of your mouth that probably (or in some cases definitely) shouldn't have. You can fill in the blank with whatever you want—the list of potential infractions gets longer every day. Whether it's a comment about someone's race, gender, sexual preference . . . or saying something that affirms biology in the face of nonsense. It could even be as simple as suggesting something the woke would agree with, but saying it at the wrong time (the need for election reform comes to mind). And the moment that it rolls off your tongue, your stomach does that little roll of horror because you realize you've just stepped into the Land of No Return. Your career—and indeed many aspects of your life—are now forfeit to the whims of an angry mob, should one choose to erupt. Depending on who heard you, you may as well go back to your desk and pack up your things: life is about to get real shitty real quick, and it's going to be that way for a while.

But why?

Whatever happened to the concept of policing our own behavior? It used to be the case that if you said something in public that offended someone, you were responsible for making it right between the two of you. Nobody else needed to stick their nose in and get involved—it was your baby. And the good thing about that was if you were the type to apologize for hurting someone's feelings and then do your best not to repeat the mistake, it really meant something. As I believe I've stated before—probably a lot—forced apologies carry very little credibility precisely because they are forced. And it's damn near impossible to tell, in this day and age, whose apologies are sincere and whose are delivered staring down the barrel of the woke gun (which will someday soon be a real gun, mark my words). When you're watching some poor bastard who let slip a racial slur when he thought a microphone wasn't on go through a Maoist-type struggle session, how in the world can you be sure whether or not he means his apology?

The answer is, you can't. And neither can the people who are screaming for his blood (not that they care to know, one way or the other). Those who have committed such infractions are admonished to "do the work" going forward, if they are to ever have any hope of redeeming themselves in the public eye. Beware the phrase "do the work," friends—behind that phrase lies eternal madness and damnation.

Because the response to people saying something wrong (and I use the word *wrong* in the loosest of senses because it isn't always something wrong) is one hundred percent arbitrary. Someone might actually "do the work" to reeducate themselves on whatever topic and reach a place where they feel that they have moved past whatever thoughts and motivations they had that arose in the situation. And if everyone around them agrees, then they're good. If everyone doesn't agree (and this is the more likely outcome), then they're consigned to continue "doing the work" ad infinitum until everyone deems them cured—which is probably never. And here's maybe the worst part: the person delivering the apology might really mean it. Some people genuinely do make mistakes and then feel bad about them. It doesn't matter, because, ultimately, the apology isn't what it's all about. It's about the example we can make of him.

This is a truly horrific picture of our society, especially when you consider that all of us have said or thought things—at one time or another—that would get us roasted on the same spit as this fellow we're describing, should we ever be caught. May the odds be ever in our favor, I guess?

Wokeism is self-aggrandizing, narcissistic, and pathological to the point of deadliness. It likes to see everything on a spectrum, except for when it doesn't—and it doesn't when it comes to what we're allowed to think. It's fashionable in our society at the moment precisely because things haven't quite gotten to the point where they've really started eating each other (though examples of this are cropping up). I would contend that the opposite of wokeism is, in fact, forgiveness, or at least the willingness to forgive.

Forgiveness requires a good-faith approach to another human being's intentions. It requires you to allow that person to be responsible for his or her own actions and for you to release some level of your own judgment. It requires humility on your part—you have to realize that you are not the arbiter of that person's fate, and you have to believe that all people have the ability to change; and that even if they don't, it's not your responsibility to lead them into thinking and speaking the right way. This doesn't mean that we don't stand up for others in the face of genuine hatred. But maybe we step off the gas pedal a bit until we've learned what that really means. Forgiveness comes down to us from the Creator—it's part of the way we're supposed to be more like Him. And if we don't learn that lesson pretty much society wide pretty soon?

The woke betide us. ★

Acknowledgments

Every author says it's impossible to thank everyone who was a part of the process of writing their book. Liars! They know exactly who made their pablum make it to the page. They just don't want to catch hell when someone thinks they should be acknowledged because they drove their school bus every morning and afternoon. "How else would you have learned to read and write?" (Thank you Ruff Reddy. . . . Yeah, that was his name.)

Thanks to Josh Jennings for doing all he could to dumb down his intellectual prowess in helping me formulate many of these thoughts. In many ways this is as much his book as it is mine.

Thanks to Alison Stonecypher for keeping her wits while I lost mine and for keeping me on track like no one else can. You're truly the sister I never had.

Thanks to Arthur Spivak and William Rodriguez, my management and agency dream team that has helped me continue to find gainful employment. It's hard for conservatives to get any love in the entertainment industry these days. You may have heard that. These guys pull off the miraculous every day.

Thanks to Frank Weimann, my literary agent, for thinking this crap was good enough to be published. Finally, someone who agreed with me.

Thanks to Humanix Books and Mary Glenn for standing in the gap and allowing conservative thought to be published and heard around the globe. You guys are the absolute best.

And finally, thanks to my BlazeTV family: Sara Gonzales, Party Foul, Steve Powell, Candice (Ortiz) Tait, Mark Tait, Hot News Natalie Stanyer, Lisa Paige, Glenn Beck, Tyler Cardon, and Gaston Mooney. You guys are the best in the biz.

Love y'all!

About the Author

Most of us are born into this world kicking and screaming, but Chad Prather most certainly came out laughing. The comedian, musician, and armchair philosopher is an unapologetic champion for anyone looking for a reason to smile. Prather's God-given gift to entertain and inspire has made him a household name, and he's grown accustomed to captivating millions of viewers on any given day.

Fans of the fast-talking, observational humorist have branded him the "modern-day Will Rogers," but if you ask Chad, he's really "just an outspoken Texan with a good heart." For Chad Prather, taking yourself too seriously is the truest form of self-sabotage, and life is too short for that!

He is the host of BlazeTV's *The Chad Prather Show* and can be found on social media wasting people's time every single day.

For booking information, email alison@watchchad.com.

Chad Prather

The Chad Prather Show podcast
watchchad.com

Facebook.com/watchchadprather

YouTube.com/chadprather1

twitter.com/watchchad

This 351-page guide will show you how to:

- Get up to $103,200 MORE in Social Security payments
- Retire overseas on $1,250 a month or less
- Create your perfect retirement plan
- Boost your income in retirement
- Save THOUSANDS on Medicare and drug costs
- Know the best age for you to start collecting Social Security
- And much, much more!

More Titles From Humanix Books You May Be Interested In:

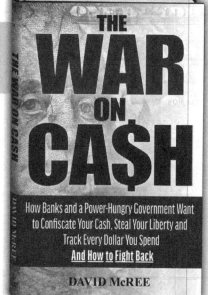

Simple **Heart Test**

Powered by Newsmaxhealth.com

FACT:

▶ Nearly half of those who die from heart attacks each year never showed prior symptoms of heart disease.

▶ If you suffer cardiac arrest outside of a hospital, you have just a 7% chance of survival.

Don't be caught off guard. Know your risk now.

TAKE THE TEST NOW ...

Renowned cardiologist **Dr. Chauncey Crandall** has partnered with **Newsmaxhealth.com** to create a simple, easy-to-complete, online test that will help you understand your heart attack risk factors. Dr. Crandall is the author of the #1 best-seller *The Simple Heart Cure: The 90-Day Program to Stop and Reverse Heart Disease.*

Take Dr. Crandall's Simple Heart Test — it takes just 2 minutes or less to complete — it could save your life!

Discover your risk now.

- **Where you score on our unique heart disease risk scale**
- Which of your lifestyle habits really protect your heart
- **The true role your height and weight play in heart attack risk**
- Little-known conditions that impact heart health
- **Plus much more!**

SimpleHeartTest.com/Crazy